Passover Desserts

Penny W. Eisenberg

IDG Books Worldwide, Inc.
An International Data Group Company

Foster City, CA ◆ Chicago, IL ◆ Indianapolis, IN ◆ New York, NY

IDG Bookds Worldwide, Inc.
An International Data Group Company
919 E. Hillsdale Boulevard
Suite 400
Foster City, CA 94404

For general information on IDG Books
Worldwide's books in the U.S., please call our
Consumer Customer Service department at
800-762-2974. For reseller information,
including discounts and premium sales, please
call our Reseller Customer Service department
at 800-434-3422.

Library of Congress Cataloging-in-Publication
Data

Eisenberg, Penny Wantuck
    Passover desserts / by Penny Wantuck
    Eisenberg.
        p. cm.
    Originally published: New York :
    Macmillan, c1996.
    Includes bibliographical references and
    index.
    ISBN 0-7645-6322-X (alk. paper)
    1. Passover cookery. 2. Desserts. I. Title.

    TX739.2.P37 E37 2001
    641.5′676—dc21   00-052982

Manufactured in the United States of America
10 9 8 7 6 5 4 3 2 1

Book design by R studio T, New York City
Cover design by Michele Laseau

$\mathscr{T}$O MY PETOO,

WHOSE LOVE AND SUPPORT HAVE NOURISHED ME

FOR TWENTY YEARS,

AND TO OUR WONDERFUL CHILDREN,

BETH AND ERIC.

ALL MY LOVE.

Contents

ACKNOWLEDGMENTS *V*

1 DIETARY GUIDELINES FOR PASSOVER *1*

2 EQUIPMENT *4*

3 INGREDIENTS *10*

4 COOKIES AND BARS *21*

5 CHEESECAKES *38*

6 PASTRY CRUSTS *51*

7 PASTRIES *62*

8 FOUNDATION CAKES *76*

9 TORTES *88*

10 LAYERED CAKES *101*

11 FROSTING, FILLINGS, AND GLAZES *129*

12 SAUCES *154*

13 FRUIT *166*

14 DECORATING BASICS *178*

APPENDIX: EQUIPMENT AND INGREDIENT SUPPLIERS *198*

BIBLIOGRAPHY *199*

INDEX *200*

$\mathscr{A}$CKNOWLEDGMENTS

I would like to thank my agent, Madeleine Morel, for believing in me and in the merit of this project. Without her, this book would probably have remained a family heirloom. My editor, Justin Schwartz, found all my mistakes and helped clarify passages that lacked precision. Projecting the concerns of the inexperienced cook, he helped me to reorganize and rewrite so that the book would work for bakers of varying experience. I am indebted to him, for his untiring efforts, for the speed with which he worked, for answering my questions and allaying my fears. Thanks also to Macmillan Publishing for bringing my dream to life. For the beautiful cover photography, thanks go to David Bishop and for the wonderful illustrations, I would like to thank Ray Skibinski.

To my parents, Roslyn and Ralph Wantuck, thank you for teaching me about good food, family, and friends and for your love and support over the years. I am grateful to Ruth and Bernie Eisenberg, for always being available to help and for always offering support and encouragement. Thanks to my sister, Karen, for help with marketing ideas and for her love over the years, and to my sister, Leslie, who always stood up for me and whose love is unending.

To my dearest friends Chris Beloni, Jackie Stutts, Lisa Wohl, Margot Blackwell, and Michelle Perlmutter (who have now tasted almost as many Passover desserts as I have), thanks for sharing the good times and the bad.

To Jeff Gleiberman, who never grew weary of my endless questions about kosher foods, and to Amalia Warshenbrot for her counsel concerning Jewish libraries and book fairs, thanks for sharing your information. My gratitude goes to Roberta Massey, for the care she has given our home, and especially my precious kitchen, over the years. Lastly, I would like to thank Linda Ingroia and IDG Books for updating and printing this paperback edition of *Passover Desserts*.

To contact me, obtain a color brochure of the desserts in this book, and find more baking tips, new recipes, and pertinent links, please visit my website at: www.pennyeisenberg.com.

1

Dietary Guidelines for Passover

Ask most Jews if there is anything that they dislike about Passover, and they invariably say, "dessert." On all other nights we eat dessert that is tasty. Why on this night do we eat desserts that look and taste like cardboard? Fortunately, we are not commanded to eat unappetizing desserts, and can change this custom if we so choose.

At Passover we eat ritual foods that are special and different from those eaten throughout the year. Dessert should be part of that wonderful tradition. Delicious and beautiful desserts that contain no forbidden foods can honor our history and make a lasting impression on our families and friends.

Celebrated in the Hebrew month of Nisan (usually April or May), Passover commemorates the exodus of the Israelites from Egypt and our deliverance from slavery. There is no other holiday in which eating plays such an important part. It is the holiday of unleavened bread, which we eat to remind us of the bread that did not have time to rise as the Israelites fled into the desert. Because we are commanded to eat matzo, and to avoid eating and even owning *hametz* (flour and water that is allowed to rise), many Jews will prepare for Passover by removing all traces of hametz from their homes. Special Passover dishes, pots and pans, and silver may be brought out. Counters may be covered with tablecloths, butcher wrapping paper, or other material to prevent them from contaminating the plates, utensils, and foods that are used only for Passover. Traditions vary greatly as to which foods may and may not be eaten. For example, most Jews will, at the very least, avoid foods with flour and leavening (except matzo). More observant Jews will also use foods that are blessed especially for Passover, and those even more strict will follow all of the guidelines outlined by their Rabbinic governing bodies. Jews from Mediterranean and Arabic countries (Sephardic Jews) eat rice and beans, while those from Germanic and Eastern European extraction strictly forbid rice and beans. There are Orthodox Jews who eat matzo, but no foods containing matzo. Vegetarians are exempt from several of the Passover guidelines, as are people with certain allergies and food sensitivities.

The guidelines that follow are excerpts (only those foods used in baking are listed) from the *Rabbinical Assembly Pesah Guide*,[1] the authority for Conservative congregations. If you have any doubts about whether or not these guidelines apply to you, consult your rabbi, and by all means make sure that your guests are aware of your practices (or cater to theirs!).

When baking, avoid the following foods:

Wheat flour (except matzo) and any foods containing flour, such as cookies or cakes

Leavening agents such as yeast, baking powder, or sourdoughs

Ashkenazic authorities also forbid the following:

All grains, except matzo and matzo products

Cornstarch, a derivative of corn

Corn syrup and any foods containing corn syrup

Legumes

Cream of tartar, because it is made during alcohol distillation

Some foods require a kosher l'Pesach label (℗ —plus the words *Kosher for Passover*, in English or Hebrew, for Orthodox Supervision; or the letter *K* and the words *Kosher for Passover* may be sufficient for those less strict) if purchased during Passover, but not if purchased before Passover. Anything purchased before Passover must be unopened.

[1] Rabbinical Assembly Pesah Guide. *Rabbinical Assembly on Jewish Law and Standards, Rabbi Mayer Rabinowitz, December 12, 1984.*

NEVER REQUIRES LABEL	REQUIRES LABEL WHENEVER PURCHASED	REQUIRES LABEL ONLY IF PURCHASED DURING PASSOVER
eggs	vanilla and other extracts (because regular extracts are made with grain alcohol)	salt (must not be iodized)
fresh fruits and vegetables	candy	spices
	yogurt	frozen fruits and juices (must not contain additives)
	alcoholic beverages	milk
	powdered sugar (must be made without cornstarch)	butter
	ice cream	baking soda
	dried fruits	nuts (peanuts are permissible)
	matzo and matzo products	cocoa
	canned or bottled juices	cream and cottage cheese
	oils (peanut oil *is* permissible)	tea
	vinegar	coffee (must not contain additives)
	soda	sugar
		honey

2

Equipment

❦ Preparing the Equipment

Baking requires a certain amount of equipment, some of which must be purchased especially for Passover, and some of which may be kashered for Passover. Here again, the rules vary and you might want to consult your own rabbi. "The process of kashering utensils depends on how the utensils are used. . . . Utensils used for cooking are kashered by boiling, those used for broiling are kashered by fire and heat and those used only for cold food are kashered by rinsing."[2]

Because baking pans cannot withstand the temperature necessary for kashering, these will have to be bought especially for Passover. Pastry brushes, rubber scrapers and other plastic items, and thermometers will also have to be bought for Passover. Other things such as measuring cups, bowls, metal spatulas, metal beaters, strainers, and sifters can probably be kashered.

The first job will be to kasher the sink. Clean the sink thoroughly. For a metal sink, pour in boiling water. For a porcelain sink, a sink rack or dish basin must be used.

The dishwasher should not be used for 24 hours, and then should run empty through a full cycle, with detergent. Thoroughly wipe down the outside and inside parts that do not get clean during the cycle.

The measuring cups, glassware, sifters, strainers, and other equipment that is used for cold food can now be run through a cycle and kashered. Metal pots and pans can be cleaned and then immersed in boiling water.

[2] Ibid.

To kasher the oven and range, clean thoroughly and then heat on the highest setting for at least a half hour. Microwave ovens should be cleaned and then a cup of water should be placed inside. The microwave should be turned on and kept on until the water evaporates. If the microwave has a browning element, it cannot be kashered.

Clean the refrigerator and freezer thoroughly, removing all hametz. Line shelves with butcher paper. If freezing food prior to Passover, don't forget to kasher the freezer beforehand.

Equipment

Suppliers of the equipment listed below can be found in the appendix (page198), source numbers below indicate those with either the best quality or the best price on the item listed.

Aluminum Foil Disposable Pans

Disposable pans, sold in supermarkets, are perfectly acceptable if you can find the right size, and do not wish to buy special pans for Passover. Follow the directions for pan preparation in each recipe even if you are substituting a disposable for the pan listed. Useful pans are the 10 × 15-inch cookie sheet, which can also be used in place of a jelly roll pan; the 8½-inch round cake pan; the 8- and 9-inch pie plate; the potato shell containers (4½ × 2¼ inches), which can be used for tarts; and the 3 × 1½-inch cupcake cups, useful for mini layered cakes.

Cake Boards

Cake boards are sturdy corrugated boards that are used to support cakes to make them easier to handle. They can be used to help remove cakes from pans and to reinvert the cakes so they are right side up. Decorated cakes are almost impossible to move unless the cake is on a board. Boards come in plain rounds, scalloped rounds, and rectangles. Rectangular boards can be cut with a sharp serrated knife. You can use a board that is a quarter-inch larger than the cake and cover the overhang with a border of frosting. This is particularly useful when you plan to store the cake on something other than the serving platter. If the cake is to be stored on the serving platter, cut the board slightly smaller than the cake so that it won't show, then pipe the bottom border directly onto the serving platter.

Cake boards are available in some craft stores, paper goods stores, and cake-decorating stores. (Sources 1, 2, and 6, page 198.)

Cake Pans

Straight-sided cake pans, available in fine cooking stores and mail-order houses, are best for layer cakes. You will not have to trim the sides of these cakes to get the layers to line up. Avoid nonstick round pans as you may damage these if sticking does occur (you might scratch the nonstick surface). Nonstick surfaces are great for rectangular pans. On these you can use a plastic turner to break away anything stuck, and then the cake should just fall out.

Springform pans should have a flat, not a fluted bottom. Don't buy inexpensive tart pans as the bottoms may warp and the sides may rust. French tart pans are excellent and are available in fine cooking stores. (Sources 1, 5, and 6, page 198.)

Food Mill

A food mill is not an essential baking tool, but it is a handy tool to have year-round. Because it is not used in cooking, it can be kashered in the dishwasher or in boiling water, so it need not be for

Passover use only. It is next to impossible to make seedless raspberry sauce without a food mill. Buy stainless steel so it won't rust.

Mixers

An expensive mixer, such as the Kitchenaid (any standing model), may seem extravagant, but it will last a lifetime and will make baking a pleasure rather than a chore. Bowls are stainless steel so they can be kashered in the dishwasher or in boiling water. They come with a flat beater, a whisk beater, and a dough hook. Extra bowls and beaters are readily available from the manufacturer. Flat beaters made completely from stainless steel are also available (as opposed to the standard enameled one) and these can be kashered. With a mixer like this there will never be a batter too thick to handle. You will save time and frustration. Good mixers can be purchased in catalog stores, department stores, and cooking stores. (Sources 1, 5, and 7, page 198.)

Parchment Paper

Parchment paper is a great way to ensure that your cakes will not stick to the pans. It is available in precut rounds (8, 9, and 10 inches) and in rolls that can be cut to fit rectangular pans. However, not all parchment is kosher. Dupont Teflon mats (source 11, page 198) are a great alternative.

Pastry Bags

For a complete description of pastry bags and other decorating paraphernalia, please see chapter 14, "Decorating Basics."

7

Pastry Brushes

Buy pastry brushes that are about one inch wide with flat bristles. When working with pastries and fruits, the bristles have to be flexible. Feather brushes are great for this, but nylon ones may be preferable for dairy desserts.

Pots

Stainless steel, enamel, or glass pots should be used when cooking eggs and acidic foods, otherwise the food may become discolored.

Rubber Scrapers

Rubber scrapers cannot be kashered for Passover. Those with plastic handles are most flexible and come in regular, half size, and extra large. The regular size will suffice.

8

Sifters

Although you can put a sifter in the dishwasher, flour particles might remain, so you would need to buy a sifter especially for Passover. A large strainer can also be used. Good sifters can be bought in supermarkets and specialty stores. Buy stainless steel so that it won't rust when it is washed.

Strainers

Medium and fine mesh strainers are both handy to have for baking. They are used to strain custards and curds and to remove unwanted material from your ingredients. Three-, six-, and eight-inch strainers are all useful. The eight-inch medium strainer can serve as a sifter. It works well because you can use it with one hand. Buy stainless steel, of course, and try to find the ones without wooden handles so that you can put them in the dishwasher or in boiling water to kasher them. (Sources 1, 5, and 7, page 198.)

Spatulas

There are many different kinds of spatulas and all of them make different aspects of baking easier. An 8-inch straight spatula (blade is 4 inches) will make frosting a cake easier. Offset spatulas are helpful in moving decorated cakes and for spreading frosting on a cake that stays in the pan. Very long spatulas work great with rectangular cakes, both for decorating and for moving them once they are decorated. Small spatulas are useful for delicate work on petits fours and other tiny cakes. Buy the best spatulas that you can afford. Good stainless steel ones will not rust and will last forever. (Sources 1, 2, and 5, page 198.)

Turntable

It is much easier to smooth the sides of a cake when you can spin the cake on a turntable. Decorating turntables are available from Sweet Celebrations (source 2, page 198), but a sturdy lazy Susan will also work.

Thermometers

There are two kinds of thermometers that are useful in baking. An instant-read thermometer gives a quick readout of temperatures under 200°F. This is handy when dealing with temperamental foods such as eggs and chocolate. A candy thermometer goes up to 400°F and has special markings for the stages that sugar goes through as it boils, such as thread, soft ball, hard ball, etc. You might want this for making buttercreams and caramels. Spend the money to buy a good-quality candy thermometer, such as Taylor (sources 1 and 2, page 198). The inexpensive ones found in super-markets may not be accurate.

3

Ingredients

Your desserts will only be as good as the ingredients you use. Equally important is the manner in which these foods are handled, combined, cooked, and stored. This section will fully acquaint you with basic ingredients as well as specialty items essential to Passover baking. The techniques described will help you make wonderful desserts, not just at Passover, but throughout the year.

Chocolate

If you cannot find Passover chocolate locally, chips are available from the Kosher Mart and block chocolate can be ordered through Gourmail (see appendix). Minimum order on the block chocolate is two 11-pound blocks, which may not be practical for the average home cook. Most of the recipes in this book are made with pareve Passover chocolate chips, because these are the easiest to find. If you have a choice, choose chocolate containing only cocoa butter, sugar, chocolate liquor, vanilla, and lecithin as these will melt the best. Under no circumstances should you buy a chocolate "baking bar," or anything that does not contain cocoa butter. This is not really even chocolate, but a chocolate-flavored coating. It has an inferior flavor and a very poor "mouth feel." Recipes that work better with bar chocolate, such as glazes, will include it.

In general (at other times of the year) chocolate chips should not be used except for recipes calling for chips, chunks, or chocolate bits, because they melt differently from regular chocolate. My favorite premium chocolates are Lindt and Callebaut, both of which have a great taste and mouth feel, but they are not available pareve and kosher for Passover.

Working with Chocolate

Chocolate will melt more evenly if it is grated or cut into small lumps. Grating chocolate in a processor makes quite a bit of noise. You might want to use earplugs.

Chocolate burns easily and should not be melted over direct heat. Instead, melt chocolate in a bowl placed *over* hot water (no higher than 140°F—not simmering). If the water is simmering, water from condensation may get into the chocolate and cause it to seize into a hard and crumbly mess. The water should not touch the bottom of the bowl so that the chocolate does not get too hot. Alternatively, chocolate can be melted in a microwave on medium power. Heat it for 30 to 60 seconds until it starts to look shiny. Stir and continue to heat in 10-second bursts until completely melted and smooth. Stir after each burst of heat. If the chocolate does seize, you might be able to fix it by adding 1 tablespoon of liquid or fat per ounce of chocolate being melted (for example, if the liquid in your recipe is water, add 1 tablespoon of water to the chocolate. If there is no liquid, add 1 tablespoon of oil per ounce of chocolate). The liquid should be the same temperature as the chocolate. Make sure that you reduce the amount of liquid or fat in the ingredients.

11

Coconut

Pasketsz brand coconut can be found in many kosher stores or can be ordered on-line (sources 3 and 9, page 198). Mounds brand coconut is a kosher product, but is not specifically produced for Passover. It is a good alternative for those who are a little more lenient with Passover dietary guidelines. Coconut tends to pack unevenly when measured in cups, which makes accuracy a problem. If possible, use the weight measurements given in each recipe.

Bakers today need to be aware of the risk of salmonella contamination from undercooked eggs. If eggs are handled properly, the risk of salmonella poisoning is very small—one case of illness per 238,500 eggs consumed.[3] To reduce risk, eggs should be brought directly home from the supermarket. They should not be stored in the little compartments in the door, but left in the carton and placed in the back of the shelf where the temperature is sure to be 40°F. Never use an egg that has a cracked shell. Because they often contain uncooked or undercooked eggs, mousses, bavarians, sabayons, and desserts of this type can present a problem if you are concerned about salmonella poisoning.

To make sure that the eggs are cooked enough to kill the bacteria, a sugar syrup boiled to 240°F can be added to the eggs. Another method is to cook the eggs to 140°F for at least 4 minutes or to 160°F for 2 to 3 seconds. All of these methods can be tricky, so follow the directions in the recipes very carefully. Because Passover is a time when we may be serving guests in high-risk categories (the elderly, infants, or those with impaired immune systems) all of the recipes in this book use one of the above methods for making sure that any salmonella will be killed.

When a recipe calls for room-temperature eggs, the eggs can be brought to room temperature quickly by immersing them, in their shells, in a bowl of warm water for several minutes. When adding sugar to eggs, gradually add it as you beat the eggs, otherwise little hard lumps of egg might form. When adding hot liquid to eggs, whisk in a little at a time so that the eggs don't cook (this is called tempering).

---

[3] Soucie, Gary, "Good Eggs," Health *magazine, May/June 1994, pp. 26–28.*

Egg Whites

Eggs are most easily separated by using an egg separator. Do each egg separately otherwise you may ruin the entire batch if you happen to have a bad egg, or if some yolk gets into the whites. Even a tiny bit of yolk mixed into whites will affect whipping. If you get a little yolk into the container you are using for separating, make sure that you discard that egg white and rinse the container before continuing to separate. Bowls, too, must be dry and grease-less or the whites may fail to whip.

For whipping egg whites to maximum volume, they should be at room temperature. To test for soft peaks, lift up the beaters slowly. If a little peak forms and the tip slumps back over, the eggs are at soft peaks. Stiff peaks stand straight up. Many recipes call for whites that are beaten "stiff but not dry." Dry eggs do not combine well with other ingredients, so that when you try to fold them in, the eggs ball up and look like little bits of Styrofoam in your batter. There are three ways to help prevent eggs from becoming dry. Cream of tartar (not allowed for Passover), whipping in a copper bowl, and adding sugar to egg whites all help to stabilize them and prevent drying. Add the sugar at the soft peak stage. Dry eggs can be remoistened using this tip from Alice Medrich: Scoop the first bit of egg whites out with a clean, grease-free spatula and see how well they blend. If overbeaten, add one unbeaten egg white to the remaining whites and beat briefly to combine.[4] This should rescue the egg whites.

13

---

[4] *Medrich, Alice*, Chocolat, *New York: Warner Books, Inc., 1990.*

Egg Yolks

Yolks are often beaten until thick and "lemony." Unbeaten yolks are bright yellow, but as they are beaten they get paler and paler. This pale color is what is meant by "lemony." When directions call for "forming a ribbon," lift up the beaters from the pale yolks and let them fall off the beater and back into the eggs. They should fall in a steady stream, a "ribbon," and then should disappear into the eggs. If the eggs fall in droplets or lumps, beat some more.

Gelatin

Kosher gelatin works differently from regular gelatin and is difficult to use in recipes where the gelatin must be liquefied and then added to cold ingredients. Bavarians, mousses, and whipped cream fall into this category. Kosher gelatin must be whisked into cold liquid and then quickly brought to a boil. It begins to set immediately and should be added to the remaining ingredients at once.

To substitute regular gelatin for kosher, mix the regular gelatin into cold liquid and let it soften for 5 minutes. Heat the gelatin until it is melted and liquid. If it is to be added to hot ingredients it can be added immediately. To add it to cold ingredients, let it stand until it is cool but still liquid and then add it to the cold ingredients. If the gelatin is not liquid enough when added, it will lump up in the finished product.

Jellies and Jams

Because jellies and jams are processed foods, they must be certified kosher for Passover. If you cannot find the exact flavor called for in a recipe, substitute one that is similar in flavor. For example, substitute strawberry or raspberry jam for currant jelly. Preserves and jams will need to be strained if they will be used for glazing. Those less strict about dietary restrictions can use any jam, jelly, or preserve that does not contain corn syrup or other restricted additives.

Margarine

It is essential to use unsalted margarine or your desserts will be salty. Do not use reduced-calorie margarine as it contains too much water and the recipes will not work properly. Remember that margarine made from corn or soybeans is not acceptable for Passover. Mother's brand margarine is made from cottonseed oil and is kosher for Passover. It does not have quite as nice a mouth feel as Fleishman's, but will do for Passover. Unless a recipe specifically says not to use butter, you can always substitute unsalted butter for the margarine and will then have the best taste possible (obviously, do not use butter if you need a pareve or low-cholesterol dessert).

Matzo Cake Meal

Matzo cake meal is sold in kosher stores, and in most grocery stores, around the time of Passover. Do not substitute matzo meal. If you cannot find it locally, call the Kosher Mart (source 3, page 198) and request Manischewitz brand matzo cake meal. This is a very finely ground, mild-tasting product perfect for baking.

Nuts

Nuts purchased before Passover do not have to be certified, even if they come in packages (make sure they are not opened before Passover). This can be very helpful if you know that you will not have access to certified nuts. Opened packages can get rancid fairly quickly, so store leftover nuts in the freezer, and make sure that you taste them before putting them in a dessert.

Skinning Hazelnuts

Kosher skinned hazelnuts can be ordered on-line (sources 3 and 9, page 198), and non-kosher can be bought through King Arthur Flour Company (source 4, page 198). To skin them yourself, place the hazelnuts on a pan in a 350°F oven and roast for 10 minutes. Pour the nuts onto the upper half of a kitchen towel. Fold the bottom half of the towel up over the nuts and rub back and forth. The skins should come off. If there are a lot of nuts with skins that won't release, place the nuts back in the oven and roast for another 5 minutes. It is okay if the nuts brown lightly. Repeat. Nuts that refuse to shed their skins can be boiled for 5 minutes and then the skins can be peeled off.

Grinding Nuts

Make sure nuts are at room temperature, otherwise they may become pasty when you try to chop them. Adding a little sugar or "flour" to them before grinding will help to absorb some of the oil released during grinding and will also prevent them from becoming pasty.

Nut Butters

As with nuts, unopened jars that do not have additives (including salt or sugar) can be purchased before Passover and require no Passover certification. Almond and cashew butters are particularly tasty. Peanut butter is acceptable for Conservative congregations.

Potato Starch

Potato starch can also be found in kosher stores and grocery stores. It is usually available all year, so make sure that the box you buy is kosher for Passover. Always smell potato starch before using, as it can spoil. If it has an unpleasant aroma, discard. If boiling the starch as a thickener, it might also be wise to see if the potato starch will gel before mixing it in with your expensive ingredients. Three tablespoons per cup of water should make a very thick gel. These recipes were made with Manischewitz brand potato starch.

Vanilla

Regular vanilla extract is not used for Passover because it contains grain alcohol. Extract prepared especially for Passover is available in some kosher stores but is not always easy to obtain. Pure, ground vanilla beans can be bought through King Arthur Flour Company (see appendix); however, they might not be suitable for everyone, because they are processed and are not certified kosher for Passover. Use ⅛ teaspoon ground vanilla beans in place of 1 teaspoon vanilla extract, and mix with dry ingredients. Vanilla beans, on the other hand, are unprocessed and do not need to be certified. Although expensive, they are readily available in supermarkets and have a wonderful flavor.

17

Working with Vanilla Beans

The best way to release the flavor of vanilla beans is to cut the bean in half lengthwise, scrape out the black seeds and put the seeds along with the beans into hot liquid. If the bean is hard, you will have to soak it in the hot liquid and then cut it. The beans can be left in the liquid for a couple of hours and then strained out. If the recipe does not call for a liquid, you can make vanilla sugar by softening a couple of vanilla beans, scraping out the seeds, and placing both the seeds and the beans into 1 pound of sugar. Let the sugar absorb the flavor for a couple of days, and then use in recipes in place of regular sugar. Vanilla sugar can be kept for at least one year. If you plan to use it for Passover the following year, make sure that you put it away so that you do not contaminate it with non-Passover utensils. If you need vanilla for a recipe that does not call for much sugar, you can follow the above method, but place the bean in only 1 cup of sugar. This will give you a very strong vanilla flavor, so that 1 or 2 teaspoons will be the equivalent of 1 teaspoon of vanilla extract. Vanilla-flavored sugar can also be found at kosher stores. These packets are usually flavored with artificial vanilla, but they are convenient.

It is possible to substitute for vanilla sugar. For each cup of vanilla sugar use regular sugar and 1 teaspoon vanilla extract, or regular sugar and a scant ⅛ teaspoon ground vanilla bean. Don't forget that if a recipe calls for vanilla extract and you are using vanilla sugar, you should add water to equal the amount of extract called for. Similarly if the recipe calls for vanilla sugar and you use extract, you should remove liquid to equal the amount of extract added.

About the Recipes ...

Within each chapter, the recipes are arranged with the pareve recipes (those containing neither dairy nor meat ingredients) first, followed by the dairy recipes. Recipes listed as dairy recipes are those that cannot be made without dairy. Unless otherwise specified, most of the pareve recipes can be made with butter if a dairy dessert is acceptable. A complete listing of dairy and pareve recipes can be found in the index.

Those recipes with a ❤ contain little or no cholesterol, but are not necessarily low in fat. For heart-healthy recipes, do not substitute butter for the margarine. A complete listing of low cholesterol as well as low fat recipes can be found in the index.

Happy baking, and Happy Pesach!

4

Cookies and Bars

Cookies and bars are wonderful for those celebrating Passover for an entire week. They make great snacks, lunchtime go-alongs, and weekday desserts. For a fancier presentation serve a platter of cookies along with a fruit dessert, mousse, or custard. Any way you eat them, they're sure to please.

HAZELNUT SANDWICH COOKIES   22

PECAN OR ALMOND SANDIES   24

COCOA COCONUT MACAROONS   25

ALMOND APRICOT PETITS FOURS   27

COCONUT AND PECAN COOKIES   30

CHEWY OR CRUNCHY ALMOND COOKIES   31

LINZER TART COOKIES   32

CHOCOLATE CHIP COOKIES   34

ORANGE GINGER SUGAR COOKIES   35

COCOA CHOCOLATE CHIP PECAN SOFTIES   36

PECAN CHOCOLATE CHIP BROWNIES   37

Hazelnut Sandwich Cookies

PAREVE

2 cups skinned hazelnuts,
page 16

1 cup sugar

2 sticks unsalted pareve Passover
margarine, room temperature

4 large egg whites, room
temperature

6 tablespoons matzo cake meal

6 tablespoons potato starch

FILLING

6 ounces pareve Passover semi-
sweet chocolate, chopped or chips

4 tablespoons pareve Passover
margarine, room temperature

1. Preheat oven to 350°F. Place oven racks on middle and low shelves of the oven. Line 2 cookie sheets with parchment paper.

2. Place the nuts and sugar in a food processor and pulse until the mixture resembles coarse meal.

3. Place the margarine in a large mixer bowl, and beat with an electric mixer until light and creamy. Add the nut-sugar mixture and beat until well mixed and light. Add the egg whites and beat for about 3 minutes more until very fluffy.

4. Sift the matzo cake meal and the potato starch together. Stir it into the above mixture until just incorporated.

Using a rounded measuring teaspoonful of dough, form mounds about the size of a marble and place these about 2 inches apart on the parchment paper. Make the mounds as round as possible so that they will be able to fit together nicely.

5. Place on the middle shelf in the oven and bake 10 to 20 minutes, until the wafer edges are well browned. If using two racks, switch the cookie sheets every 5 minutes so that all the cookies bake evenly (the time will depend on the type of oven, type of cookie sheet, and how many sheets and ovens you are using).

6. Remove the parchment paper to a cooling rack and let the cookies cool completely on the parchment paper. The cookies should be crisp when cool. If they aren't, return them to the oven for 5 minutes.

7. For the filling, bring 2 inches of water to boil in the bottom of a double boiler. Remove from heat.

8. Chop the chocolate and margarine into 1-inch chunks. Place in the top of the double boiler, or into a metal bowl that will fit the bottom boiler, and place over the hot, but not simmering water. Stir until melted and smooth. Let cool to room temperature.

9. To assemble: Spread the flat side of a cookie with a thin layer of chocolate and top with the flat side of another cookie. Repeat with the remaining cookies.

Can Prepare Ahead

REFRIGERATED, 1 DAY; FROZEN, 3 MONTHS

Makes 3½ dozen 2-inch cookies

Pecan or Almond Sandies

PAREVE

³/₄ cup pecans or almonds

¹/₂ cup sugar

¹/₄ cup potato starch

1¹/₄ cups matzo cake meal

1¹/₂ teaspoons Passover vanilla
  extract or substitute

1¹/₂ sticks unsalted pareve
  Passover margarine, cold

1. Preheat oven to 350°F. Line two cookie sheets with parchment paper.

2. Process the nuts, sugar, potato starch, and matzo cake meal in a food processor with a metal blade, until the nuts are finely ground.

3. Add the vanilla extract. Cut the margarine into tablespoon-size chunks and add to the work bowl. Process until the mixture forms a dough. It will not completely ball up, but will start to stick together.

4. Roll the dough into balls, approximately 1¼ inches in diameter. Place the balls on the parchment paper. Press down on each ball with the back of a measuring cup (cover the dough with a piece of parchment if the dough sticks) until the dough is about ⅛ inch thick.

5. With a sharp knife, crosshatch (like a tic-tac-toe) the cookies. Place in the refrigerator or freezer for 15 minutes.

6. Set the cookie sheets on the middle shelf in the oven and bake cookies 15 to 25 minutes until lightly browned (almond cookies will brown very little). Slide the parchment onto a wire rack so the cookies can cool.

Can Prepare Ahead

REFRIGERATED, 2 DAYS; FROZEN, 3 MONTHS

Makes 2¹/₂ dozen 3-inch cookies

PAREVE

1 fourteen-ounce package
(3¼ cups) coconut flakes

2 tablespoons matzo cake meal

2 tablespoons unsweetened cocoa
powder

1 cup sugar

4 large egg whites

Cocoa Coconut Macaroons

THESE MACAROONS BEAR NO RESEMBLANCE TO THE
SWEET, STICKY COOKIES THAT COME OUT OF PASSOVER
TINS. INSTEAD, THEY ARE MOIST AND CHEWY WITH THE
FLAVORS OF COCONUT AND COCOA SHINING THROUGH.
FOR AN EXTRA SPECIAL TOUCH, DIP OR DRIZZLE WITH
CHOCOLATE.

1. Preheat oven to 375°F. Put parchment paper on one or two
cookie sheets.

2. Place the coconut, matzo cake meal, and cocoa in a food
processor and pulse on and off until the coconut is finely ground.

3. Combine the sugar and egg whites in a metal mixing bowl that
will fit over a double boiler (or in the top of the double boiler).
Bring about 2 inches of water to boil in the bottom of the boiler,
and set the bowl over the simmering water. Whisk lightly, but
constantly, until the eggs are about 110°F (warm, but not hot, to
the touch). Remove from the heat and continue to whisk-stir until
the sugar has dissolved.

Add the sugar mixture to the coconut in the food processor and
pulse to blend together.

4. Use a pastry bag with an extra-large star tip (6–8B) or cut a
1-inch hole in the end of a pastry bag. Onto the parchment-lined
sheets, pipe out mounds that are 1½ inches in diameter and
1½ inches high. With your fingers, shape the tip to a point to make
the traditional "kiss"-shaped macaroon. Alternatively the
batter can be spooned onto the sheets using a tablespoon.

5. Place on the middle shelf in the oven and bake for 13 to 15 minutes or until the crust dulls. If using more than one cookie sheet, use the middle and lower racks, cook for 7½ minutes, and then switch the positions of the trays.

Can Prepare Ahead

REFRIGERATED, 1 DAY; FROZEN, 3 MONTHS

Makes 24 1½-inch cookies

Almond Apricot Petits Fours

MUST BE MADE 1 DAY AHEAD

PAREVE

8 ounces Passover almond paste

$^1/_2$ cup sugar

8 tablespoons (1 stick) unsalted pareve Passover margarine, at room temperature

3 level tablespoons honey

4 large eggs, room temperature

$^3/_8$ cup matzo cake meal

$^3/_8$ cup potato starch

$^1/_4$ teaspoon salt

FILLING

1 twelve-ounce jar apricot or seedless raspberry jam

TOPPING

$2^1/_2$ ounces pareve Passover semi-sweet chocolate, chopped or chips

2 teaspoons mild vegetable oil

1. Preheat oven to 400°F. Grease two 10 × 15-inch jelly roll pans. Place parchment paper on the bottom of each.

2. Place the almond paste and the sugar in a food processor and process until the almond paste is finely ground into the sugar. Transfer to a large mixer bowl.

3. Add the margarine and mix on low to blend. Add the honey and eggs and beat on medium high until pale in color and fluffy, about 5 minutes.

4. Sift the matzo cake meal, potato starch, and salt together and then stir into the almond paste mixture (with a heavy-duty mixer you can mix in the dry ingredients on low).

5. Divide the batter between the pans and spread it with an offset spatula so that each layer is about $^1/_8$ inch thick.

Place one of the pans on the middle shelf in the oven and bake 5 minutes or until the top of the cake looks dry (the cake will not be brown).

6. Remove from the oven and place on a wire cooling rack. Bake the remaining cake using the above instructions and cool on a wire cooling rack. Run a knife around the outside of each cake to loosen the edges. Place a piece of waxed paper on the top of each layer and cover with a cake board (the same size or larger than the cake). Hold the board to the pan and flip the pan over so that the cake transfers to the waxed paper–covered board. Repeat with the other cake.

7. Cut both cakes in half to form four layers, each 9 × 7½ inches. Cut through the waxed paper. Place cake boards under three of the layers and place them in the freezer.

8. Heat the jam and strain it (raspberry does not need to be strained—use a wire whisk to smooth it out). Spread ⅓ of the jam (about ⅓ cup) over one layer. Retrieve one of the layers from the freezer and slide it on top of the jam. The jam will make the cakes slippery so you will be able to move the cake if it didn't slide onto the right place. The cake will also be trimmed so you needn't worry if you didn't cut them exactly in half. Repeat with the remaining layers. The top will have no jam on it.

9. Slide the waxed paper with the cake on it onto a cookie sheet. Cover with plastic wrap. Let stand at room temperature for ½ hour to thaw the layers. Place a jelly roll or other pan (at least as large as the cake) on top of the plastic wrap. Put two 5-pound packages of flour, aluminum cans, or other weights in the pan to weight down the cake (do not put the weights directly on the cake as you will end up with a ripply cake). Refrigerate overnight.

10. The next day boil 2 inches of water in the bottom of a double boiler. Reduce heat so water is just under a simmer. In the top of the double boiler or in a bowl that will fit the pan, place the chocolate and oil. Place over the hot water, and heat until the chocolate melts. Stir to blend the chocolate and oil together.

11. Spread the melted chocolate over the cake, quickly and as smoothly as possible (an offset cake-decorating spatula works well). It will not seem that there is enough chocolate, but you want it to be very thin or the chocolate will overpower the other flavors.

12. While the chocolate is still melted, decorate with a dessert fork. Lefties should start at the right and righties at the left side of the cake. Hold the fork almost parallel to the surface of the cake. Press the tines to the chocolate and gently pull up. Repeat this going either down or across the cake, leaving a tiny space between tine marks. Try to make the marks in rows so that the design will look nice once the squares are cut. If the chocolate is still melted when you are done decorating, refrigerate the cake for 5 minutes to firm up the chocolate a little.

13. Trim the edges off of the cake and then cut the cake into squares, slightly larger than 1 inch (see "Cutting Cakes," page 189). If the chocolate starts to crack as you cut it, let it stand at room temperature until it warms slightly and can be cut without cracking.

Can Prepare Ahead

———

REFRIGERATED, 2 DAYS; FROZEN, 3 MONTHS

Makes 30 to 40 squares

Coconut and Pecan Cookies

2 cups matzo cake meal

1 cup kosher for Passover potato flakes

1 cup loosely packed coconut flakes

1 cup (2 sticks) unsalted pareve Passover margarine, room temperature, cut into tablespoons

1 cup packed brown sugar

1 cup sugar

1 tablespoon water

2 level tablespoons honey

2 large egg yolks, room temperature

1/2 cup pecans, coarsely chopped

30

1. Preheat oven to 375°F. Line cookie sheets with parchment paper.

2. Place the matzo cake meal, potato flakes, and coconut in a food processor and pulse a few times to grind ingredients into smaller pieces.

3. In a large mixer bowl, beat the margarine until creamy. Add both sugars and beat until well blended. Add the water, honey, and egg yolks and beat on low to incorporate. Stir in the dry ingredients (from the processor) and the pecans.

4. Shape the dough into 1½-inch balls (about the size of a walnut) and place on the parchment paper (if the dough is too dry to hold together, add up to 1 teaspoon of water, just until the dough can be patted into a ball). Flatten balls with the bottom of a cup until the dough resists and the cookies are about 2 inches in diameter and about ¼ inch thick.

5. Place on the middle shelf in the oven and bake for 12 to 14 minutes until well browned but still very soft. If using two trays, bake for 6 minutes, switch the positions of the trays, and bake for 6 to 7 more minutes. Let the cookies cool on the parchment paper on wire racks.

Can Prepare Ahead

REFRIGERATED, 1 DAY; FROZEN, 3 MONTHS

Makes 2 1/2 to 3 dozen 3-inch cookies

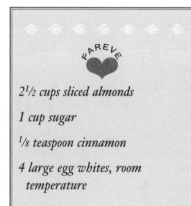

2¹/₂ cups sliced almonds

1 cup sugar

¹/₈ teaspoon cinnamon

4 large egg whites, room
temperature

Chewy or Crunchy Almond Cookies

1. Preheat oven to 325°F. Place parchment paper on cookie sheets.

2. Place the almonds, sugar, and cinnamon in a food processor bowl. Pulse on and off until the almonds are ground to a powder. Add the egg whites and pulse until the mixture forms a dough.

3. Drop the dough by teaspoonful onto the cookie sheets. For chewy cookies: place on the middle shelf in the oven and bake for 15 minutes. For crunchy cookies: place on the middle shelf in the oven and bake 20 minutes, reduce heat to 200°F and bake for 2 hours. Instead of reducing the heat, you can turn the heat off, and leave the cookies in the oven overnight.

Can Prepare Ahead

Chewy: REFRIGERATED, 1 DAY; FROZEN, 3 MONTHS

Crunchy: REFRIGERATED, 1 WEEK; FROZEN, 3 MONTHS

Makes 2 dozen

31

PAREVE

2 cups unsalted blanched almonds, slivered or sliced

3 cups matzo cake meal

1 cup sugar

1 teaspoon cinnamon

1/2 teaspoon ground cloves

3 sticks unsalted, pareve Passover margarine, softened and cut into pieces

3 tablespoons honey

1 large egg yolk

1 tablespoon water

1 large egg white, whisked with 1 teaspoon water

1/4 cup finely chopped almonds

1/2 cup seedless raspberry jam

Linzer Tart Cookies

BAKERY LINZER TART COOKIES ARE LARGE PALE COOKIES, FILLED WITH RASPBERRY JAM. THIS RECIPE IS MORE LIKE THE ORIGINAL AUSTRIAN LINZERTORTE, SPICED WITH CINNAMON AND CLOVE AND BAKED UNTIL JUST BEGINNING TO BROWN. EGGS AND HONEY HAVE BEEN ADDED TO GIVE FLAVOR AND BODY TO THIS FLOURLESS VERSION. DON'T SUBSTITUTE BUTTER FOR THE MARGARINE. THE TEXTURE IS BEST WHEN MADE WITH MARGARINE.

1. Preheat oven to 350°F. Line several cookie sheets with parchment paper.

PROCESSOR METHOD—REQUIRES A 6-CUP PROCESSOR

2. Place the almonds, cake meal, sugar, cinnamon, and cloves in a processor bowl and using the metal blade, process until the almonds are finely ground. Add the margarine, honey, egg yolk, and water and pulse until the dough is well mixed, about 25 seconds.

MIXER METHOD

2. Place the nuts, 1/4 cup matzo cake meal, cinnamon, and cloves in a processor and pulse on and off until the nuts are finely ground. In a large mixer bowl, beat the margarine until creamy. Add the sugar a little at a time and beat until well blended. Beat in the honey, egg yolk, and water, just to blend together. Stir in the almonds and remaining matzo cake meal until well blended.

EITHER METHOD

3. Turn the dough out onto a pastry board or piece of waxed paper, and press it into a single mass. Divide it into quarters, remove 1 quarter, and place the rest in a plastic bag or covered bowl. Using a rolling pin, roll the piece between waxed paper to a little less than ⅛ inch. Cut with a 2-inch round or fluted cookie cutter.

4. Cut a ½-inch hole in the center of half of the cookies. To remove the hole, lift the cookie up with a wide spatula. Slide it onto your fingers and spread your fingers so that the hole cutout drops through them while the cookie is supported by your fingers. Place the cookie on the prepared cookie sheets. Brush the tops (the ones with the holes) with a little of the egg white and sprinkle with chopped nuts.

5. Place on the middle shelf in the oven and bake cookies 13 to 17 minutes, until lightly browned. Slide the parchment onto a rack and let the cookies cool. Repeat with the remaining dough.

6. When the cookies are cool, place a scant teaspoon of raspberry jam in the center of each bottom, and top with a cookie with a hole in it. Press down lightly to spread the jam to the edges of the cookie.

Can Prepare Ahead

REFRIGERATED, 1 DAY; FROZEN, 3 MONTHS

Cookies are crisp when first made but get softer as they sit. Refrigerate in an airtight container. Freeze cookies with waxed paper between layers.

Makes 4 dozen cookies

33

Chocolate Chip Cookies

1⅓ cups chopped pecans

1¾ cups brown sugar

½ cup matzo cake meal

½ cup potato starch

5 large egg whites

¾ cup pecans, coarsely chopped

2 ounces pareve Passover semi-sweet chocolate chips

1. Preheat oven to 400°F. Grease 2 baking sheets, line with parchment paper, and grease the paper.

2. Combine the pecans, brown sugar, matzo cake meal, and potato starch in a processor and pulse on and off until the nuts are finely grated. Add the egg whites and pulse to blend.

3. Transfer the batter to a bowl and stir in the nuts and chocolate. Let the batter sit for 10 minutes to thicken.

4. Drop the batter by rounded tablespoonfuls onto the parchment paper–lined cookie sheets, leaving 1 inch between cookies. Place one sheet on the middle and one sheet on the lower shelf. Bake for 4 minutes. Switch the lower sheet to the top and vice versa. Bake for 4 minutes more. The cookies should be dull, but very soft. If not dull, bake for 1 more minute. Transfer the parchment to a cooling rack, and let the cookies cool before storing.

Can Prepare Ahead

REFRIGERATED, 1 DAY; FROZEN, 3 MONTHS

Makes 2½ dozen 2½-inch cookies

34

Orange Ginger Sugar Cookies

1⅓ cups sugar

2 tablespoons potato starch

12 tablespoons (1½ sticks)
unsalted pareve Passover
margarine, room temperature

1 tablespoon ground ginger

1 teaspoon ground cinnamon

2 tablespoons fresh orange juice

2 large egg yolks, room
temperature

2 cups matzo cake meal

1. Preheat oven to 375°F.

2. Place the sugar and the potato starch in the work bowl of a processor and process until the sugar is finely ground. Add the margarine, ginger, and cinnamon and process until well blended. Add the egg yolks and orange juice and process to blend.

3. Add the matzo flour and pulse until the flour disappears. Shape the dough into balls, 1¼ inches in diameter. Roll the balls in sugar and place on parchment-lined cookie sheets. Press the cookies with the bottom of a measuring cup until ⅛ inch thick.

4. Place on the middle shelf in the oven and bake for 15 minutes, or until very nicely browned. Remove the parchment to wire racks and let the cookies cool before storing.

Can Prepare Ahead

REFRIGERATED, 1 DAY; FROZEN, 3 MONTHS

Makes 3 dozen 2-inch cookies

35

VARIATION

Lemon Nutmeg Cookies: Substitute 2 teaspoons of freshly grated nutmeg for the ginger, and omit the cinnamon. Use lemon juice instead of orange juice.

Cocoa Chocolate Chip Pecan Softies

1½ cups chopped pecans

2 cups sugar

½ cup unsweetened cocoa

¼ cup matzo cake meal

¼ cup potato starch

5 large egg whites

¾ cup pecans, coarsely chopped

¾ cup pareve Passover semisweet chocolate chips

36

VARIATION

For a low-fat cookie (1 gram each), omit the coarsely chopped pecans and the chocolate chips. Bake the cookies 9 to 10 minutes.

1. Preheat oven to 400°F. Line two cookie sheets with parchment paper.

2. Combine the 1½ cups of pecans, sugar, cocoa powder, matzo cake meal, and potato starch in a processor and pulse on and off until the nuts are finely grated. Add the egg whites and pulse to blend.

3. Transfer the batter to a bowl and stir in the remaining nuts and chocolate. Let the batter sit for 10 minutes to thicken.

4. Drop the batter by well-rounded teaspoonfuls (use regular spoon, not measuring spoon) onto the parchment paper cookie sheets leaving 1 inch between cookies.

5. Place one sheet on the middle and one sheet on the lower shelf. Bake for 4 minutes. Switch the lower sheet to the top and vice versa. Bake for 4 minutes more. The cookies should be dull, but very soft. If not dull, bake for 1 more minute. Transfer the parchment to a cooling rack, and let the cookies cool before storing.

Can Prepare Ahead

REFRIGERATED, 2 DAYS; FROZEN, 3 MONTHS

Makes 2½ dozen 2½-inch cookies

Pecan Chocolate Chip Brownies

10 tablespoons (1¼ sticks) unsalted pareve Passover margarine, plus 1 teaspoon for greasing pan

6 ounces pareve Passover semi-sweet chocolate chips

1⅛ cups vanilla sugar, or substitute, page 18

1½ teaspoons water

3 large eggs, room temperature

¾ cup matzo cake meal

¾ cup pecan pieces

¾ cup pareve Passover semisweet chocolate chips

1. Preheat oven to 350°F. Grease an 8-inch square pan with margarine and sprinkle with matzo cake meal.

2. Melt the margarine in a medium saucepan over low heat. Remove from heat, add 6 ounces chocolate chips, and stir until they are melted. Whisk in the sugar and the water or vanilla extract. Test the temperature of the chocolate. It should be tepid. If it is not, let it rest until it is tepid.

3. Whisk the eggs together and then add them to the chocolate, constantly whisking until they are well mixed in. Using a wooden spoon, stir in the matzo cake meal until blended. Add the nuts and remaining chocolate chips. Spread the batter in the prepared pan.

4. Place on the middle shelf in the oven and bake 25 to 30 minutes, until a toothpick inserted in the center comes out with a moist crumb. Cool completely on a wire rack. Loosen the sides with a plastic spatula and then invert the brownies onto a cake board or cutting board. Reinvert so brownies are right side up. Cut into 9 pieces. They will taste different if eaten at room temperature or cold, so experiment to see which you prefer.

37

Can Prepare Ahead

REFRIGERATED, 1 DAY; FROZEN, 3 MONTHS

Makes 9 brownies or one 9-inch round

5

Cheesecakes

Cheesecake, a favorite dessert for many Americans, should not be overlooked for Passover week. For those who don't keep kosher, the Lemon Chocolate Marbled Cheesecake Squares, Chocolate Almond Cheesecake Bars, and the Caramel Cheesecake Squares are perfect for the conclusion of the Seder meal. They are also wonderful for Onegs and other gatherings. Together with the strawberry and cherry versions, these cheesecakes are wonderful dairy desserts for those special occasions that fall during Passover. For year-round pleasure, substitute regular crumb crusts for the Passover version and use the fillings as written. Your guests will be thrilled.

STRAWBERRY SOUR CREAM CHEESECAKE   39

CARAMEL CHEESECAKE SQUARES   42

CHERRY CHEESECAKE   44

CHOCOLATE ALMOND CHEESECAKE BARS   46

LEMON CHOCOLATE MARBLED CHEESECAKE SQUARES   49

Strawberry Sour Cream Cheesecake

BAKING CHEESECAKE IN A WATER BATH PROVIDES GENTLE HEAT THAT HELPS TO KEEP THE OUTER EDGE OF THE CHEESECAKE FROM OVERBAKING. THIS MAKES FOR A SMOOTH CHEESECAKE THROUGHOUT. THE SOUR CREAM PROVIDES JUST THE RIGHT AMOUNT OF TARTNESS TO COMPLEMENT THE STRAWBERRIES.

1 recipe "Graham Cracker" Crust, page 53 (can prepare 1 week in advance)

FILLING

16 ounces cream cheese, room temperature

2 cups sour cream

1½ cups vanilla sugar or substitute, page 18

¼ cup half-and-half

3 large eggs, room temperature

3 large egg yolks, room temperature

TOPPING

1 recipe Strawberry Filling, page 143

1 pint strawberries

1. Preheat oven to 350°F. Have a 12-inch square or 12 × 15-inch baking pan nearby, and set a teakettle full of water on the burner on high heat. When the water comes to boiling, turn the burner to low to keep the water simmering. This will be used for a water bath (*bain marie*).

2. To prevent water from seeping into the springform, it must be wrapped in aluminum foil. To do this, tear off four sheets of heavy-duty aluminum foil, each 17 inches long, and stack them one on top of the other.

3. Fold down ½ inch of a long side. Repeat two times. Open up the foil so that the fold is in the middle. You will have two layers of foil on each side of the fold. Tape the outside of the fold with waterproof tape. Wrap the foil around the outside of a 9- or 10-inch springform pan and crimp the top edge so that the foil will stay on the pan, but will not interfere with the crust.

4. Butter the springform and then pack the crumb mixture onto the bottom and ¾ of the way up the sides of the pan (you can use your index finger as a guide by measuring down from the top of the pan the length of one joint).

PROCESSOR METHOD—REQUIRES A 6-CUP PROCESSOR

5. Place the cream cheese in a processor bowl and process until smooth. Add the sour cream and pulse to blend. Add the sugar and extract, if using, and pulse until blended. Add the half-and-half to the bowl and pulse to combine. Add the eggs and yolks and pulse a couple of times until the eggs are incorporated. Scrape down the bowl and pulse a couple more times to blend.

MIXER METHOD

5. Place the cream cheese in a large mixer bowl and beat on medium speed until creamy. Add the sugar and beat until well blended with the cheese. Add the sour cream and half-and-half, and beat until incorporated into the cheese. Lastly add the eggs and yolks and beat on low speed just to blend together.

TO CONTINUE

6. Pour the filling into the crust. Place the springform into the larger pan. Pour the boiling water carefully around the springform until it comes halfway up the sides of the springform.

7. Place on the middle shelf in the oven and bake 1 hour and 10 minutes. Turn off the heat and let cake rest in the oven for 45 minutes. Remove from the oven and let cool to room temperature. Remove the springform from the water bath, cover the cheesecake with foil, and refrigerate overnight or up to three days ahead of serving.

Make the topping and let cool uncovered. Use at once or cover and refrigerate until ready to use.

8. Up to one day before serving, wash the berries, pat dry, and cut off the stems. Brush the bottom of the berries with some of the strawberry filling. Place the whole berries around the outside edge of the cake. Fill the center with the strawberry filling, reserving a couple of tablespoons for glazing. Use a pastry brush to glaze the berries. Refrigerate until ready to serve.

Can Prepare Ahead

Cheesecake without topping:
REFRIGERATED, 3 DAYS; FROZEN, 3 MONTHS
Strawberry topping: REFRIGERATED, 2 DAYS
Finished cake: REFRIGERATED, 1 DAY

Makes 8 to 12 servings

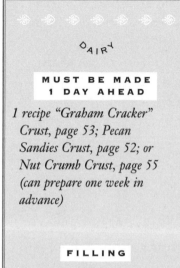

MUST BE MADE 1 DAY AHEAD

1 recipe "Graham Cracker" Crust, page 53; Pecan Sandies Crust, page 52; or Nut Crumb Crust, page 55 (can prepare one week in advance)

FILLING

24 ounces cream cheese, at room temperature

1 cup whipping cream

1 cup vanilla sugar or substitute, page 18

3 large eggs

3 large egg yolks

TOPPING

1 recipe Caramel Topping, page 146

42

Caramel Cheesecake Squares

THIS RECIPE WILL PRODUCE SQUARES OF VARYING TEXTURES, RANGING FROM CREAMY TO DRY. THIS IS NICE BECAUSE PEOPLE HAVE DIFFERENT IDEAS ABOUT WHAT MAKES A GREAT CHEESECAKE.

1. Preheat oven to 350°F. Grease the sides of a 9 × 13-inch baking pan. Place a double layer of heavy-duty aluminum foil in the pan with the long sides extending 3 inches over the pan. Pack the crumbs into the bottom of the pan.

FOOD PROCESSOR METHOD—REQUIRES A 6-CUP PROCESSOR

2. Place the cream cheese and the cream in a processor bowl and process until the mixture is smooth. Add the sugar, and extract if you are using it, and process until well mixed. Add the eggs and the egg yolks and pulse together a few times until blended.

MIXER METHOD

2. Place the cream cheese in a large mixer bowl and beat on medium speed until creamy. Add the sugar and beat until well blended with the cheese. Add the cream and beat until incorporated into the cheese. Lastly, add the eggs and beat on low speed just to blend together.

TO CONTINUE

3. Pour the mixture into the crust. Place on the middle shelf in the oven and bake 45 to 50 minutes, until the top looks dull. The center of the cheesecake should not "shake" when you move the pan. If in doubt, err on the side of underdone, which will yield a

If you prefer to have all of the squares creamy, bake in a bain marie *(water bath—see the directions with the Lemon Chocolate Marbled Cheesecake Squares, page 49).*

creamier cheesecake, as opposed to overdone, which will be dry and lifeless. Let cool completely on a wire rack.

4. Prepare the Caramel Topping and pour over the cooled cheesecake. Cool to room temperature and then refrigerate overnight.

5. Use a small knife or spatula to free the short ends of the cheesecake. Lift the cheesecake by the extended foil and set it on a cutting board.

6. To cut the cheesecake, use a long nonserrated knife. Begin by cutting ¼ inch off all sides. Along the long side, measure off 2-inch segments. Cut through the cake and then wiggle the knife side to side to separate the pieces and make room for the knife to come out without marring the surface of the caramel. Wipe the blade with a warm, damp cloth after each cut. You will have strips that are 2 inches wide and 8½ inches long. The last strip will only be 1½ inches wide. It can be set aside or cut into 1½-inch squares. Cut the other strips into 2-inch squares. If desired the squares can be cut in half to form triangles.

When storing, make sure that the container cover does not touch the caramel or the surface will become marred. If frozen, the crust will get a little soggy.

Can Prepare Ahead

—

REFRIGERATED, 4 DAYS; FROZEN, 3 MONTHS

Makes twenty 2-inch squares

Cherry Cheesecake

THIS CHERRY CHEESECAKE IS SLIGHTLY UNUSUAL BECAUSE OF THE CINNAMON, ORANGE JUICE, AND PASSOVER WINE IN THE CHERRY FILLING. THE FLAVORS WORK BEAUTIFULLY WITH THE SWEET, RICH CHEESECAKE FILLING.

1. Preheat oven to 350°F. Butter the sides, and then press the crumb mixture onto the bottom and ¾ of the way up the sides of a 9- or 10-inch springform pan. Use the first joint of your index finger as a guide, down from the top of the form.

PROCESSOR METHOD—REQUIRES A 6-CUP PROCESSOR

2. Place the cream cheese and half-and-half in a processor bowl and process until smooth. Add the sugar, and extract if you are using it, and process until well mixed. Add the eggs and the egg yolks and pulse together a few times until everything is blended. Pour the mixture into the crust.

MIXER METHOD

2. Place the cream cheese in a large mixer bowl and beat on medium speed until creamy. Add the sugar and beat until well blended with the cheese. Add the half-and-half and beat until incorporated into the cheese. Lastly, add the eggs and yolks and beat on low speed just to blend together.

DAIRY

1 recipe "Graham Cracker" Crust, page 53 (can prepare 1 week in advance)

FILLING

20 ounces cream cheese, at room temperature

¾ cup half-and-half

¾ cup vanilla sugar or substitute, page 18

3 large eggs

2 large egg yolks

TOPPING

1 recipe Marinated Cherry Filling, page 141

44

To Continue

3. Pour the mixture into the crust. Place on the middle shelf in the oven and bake 45 to 50 minutes, until the top looks dull. The center of the cheesecake should not "shake" when you move the pan. Remove from the oven.

4. Punch some holes in a piece of aluminum foil to allow steam to escape and then loosely cover the top of the cake with the foil. Let cool to room temperature. Refrigerate overnight or up to 2 days ahead.

5. Make the topping and refrigerate until cold. Just before serving, spoon on the topping.

The cheesecake will keep in the refrigerator for 1 week, but will look prettiest within a day or two of adding the topping.

Can Prepare Ahead

REFRIGERATED, 2 DAYS

Makes 8 to 12 servings

Chocolate Almond Cheesecake Bars

TASTING LIKE THEY ARE LACED WITH AMARETTO LIQUEUR, YET COMPLETELY KOSHER FOR PASSOVER, THESE BARS BRING RAVE REVIEWS YEAR-ROUND. THEY ARE SURE TO BECOME A FAMILY FAVORITE.

DAIRY

1 recipe Pecan Sandies Cookie Crust (page 52), using almonds instead of pecans (can prepare 1 week in advance)

FILLING

8 ounces Passover almond paste

1½ cups vanilla sugar or substitute, page 18

9 ounces semisweet Passover chocolate chips

24 ounces cream cheese, room temperature

¾ cup half-and-half

4 large eggs, room temperature

3 large egg yolks, room temperature

DECORATIONS

2 ounces Passover white or dark chocolate, grated

1 teaspoon mild vegetable oil

1. Preheat oven to 350°F. Grease the sides of a 9 × 13-inch baking pan. Place a piece of parchment paper in the bottom of the pan, and grease it. Pack the crust crumbs into the bottom of the pan.

2. Crumble the almond paste into the bowl of a food processor. Add the sugar and process until the almond paste is finely ground into the sugar.

3. Put the chocolate in the top of a double boiler. Place over hot, but not simmering water, and let the chocolate melt (for microwave method, see page 11). Add the chocolate to the work bowl and pulse to blend ingredients together. If using vanilla extract, add it now.

4. Place the cream cheese in a mixer bowl and beat on medium speed until the cheese is soft and creamy. Add the sugar/chocolate mixture and beat until well blended. Scrape down the bowl.

5. Add the half-and-half a little at a time and beat on low until well blended. Mix the eggs and yolks and stir with a fork to blend. Add to the cream cheese a little at a time as you beat on low just to blend. Scrape down the bowl and beat a few times to combine.

6. Pour the batter over the crust. Place on the middle shelf in the oven and bake for 40 to 45 minutes, until the edges are firm and the top is dull. If in doubt, err on the undercooked side as the cake will taste better if it is a little creamier, rather than a little drier.

7. Remove from oven. Perforate a piece of aluminum foil in 12 to 15 places using a skewer, and then cover the cheesecake loosely with the foil. Cool on a rack to room temperature. Refrigerate overnight.

8. Use a small knife or spatula to free the edges of the cheesecake. Place a cake board over the cheesecake and invert. Use another cake board or a cutting board to reinvert the cheesecake so that it is right side up.

9. To cut the cheesecake use a long nonserrated knife. Begin by cutting ¼ inch off all sides. Along the long side, measure off 2-inch segments. Cut through the cake and then wiggle the knife side to side to separate the pieces and make room for the knife to come out without marring the surface of the cheesecake. Wipe the blade with a warm, damp cloth after each cut.

10. You will now have strips that are 2 inches wide and 8½ inches long. The last strip will only be 1½ inches wide. It can be set aside or cut into 1½-inch squares. Cut the other strips into 2-inch squares. Two-inch squares are a nice size if serving alone. If serving as part of a buffet table, the squares can be cut in half to form triangles (and for petit four size the triangles can again be cut in half) or you can make 1-inch squares. The cake also looks nice if you cut many different shapes and arrange the shapes on a platter.

DECORATIONS

11. Heat the chocolate and oil in the microwave on medium for 30 to 60 seconds until the chocolate begins to melt and looks shiny. Stir. Continue to heat in 10-second bursts, stirring between heating until the chocolate is completely melted and the mixture is smooth.

12. Pipe or drizzle the chocolate over the squares diagonally, from corner to corner, with an "s" or snake pattern. Use the decoration to hide imperfections in the surface of the cheesecake. Refrigerate for 1 hour to firm the chocolate. Serve cold.

Can Prepare Ahead

REFRIGERATED, 3 DAYS; FROZEN, 3 MONTHS

Makes twenty 2-inch squares

Lemon Chocolate Marbled Cheesecake Squares

DAIRY

MUST BE MADE 1 DAY AHEAD

1 recipe "Graham Cracker" Crust, page 53 (can be prepared 1 week in advance)

FILLING

21 ounces cream cheese, room temperature

1 cup vanilla sugar or substitute, see page 18

1 cup sour cream

⅓ cup half-and-half

1 to 2 tablespoons fresh lemon juice (about 1 lemon) or to taste

1 tablespoon lemon zest, optional

4 large eggs, room temperature

2 large egg yolks, room temperature

DECORATIONS

2 ounces Passover semisweet chocolate, chopped, or chips

1. Preheat oven to 300°F. Have a 12 × 15-inch baking pan nearby. Heat water in a teakettle until boiling. Turn heat to low to keep the water simmering (to be used for a water bath). Grease the sides of a 9 × 13-inch baking pan. Place a double layer of heavy-duty aluminum foil in the pan with the long sides extending 3 inches over the pan. Press the crumbs into the bottom of the smaller pan.

2. Place the cream cheese in a mixer bowl and beat until the cheese is soft and creamy. Add the sugar and mix on medium to medium-high speed until the sugar and cheese are well blended.

3. Add the sour cream and beat on low until well blended. Scrape down bowl, add the half-and-half and vanilla extract, if you are using it, and beat on low to blend. For a lightly scented lemon cake, use 1 tablespoon lemon juice and 1 teaspoon zest. For more robust flavor, add the remaining juice and zest, or to taste. Beat on low to blend.

4. Combine the eggs and yolks and stir with a fork to blend. Add to the cheese mixture and beat on low until well blended. Scrape down bowl and beat to blend. Remove 1 cup of batter and spoon the remainder over the crust.

5. Melt chocolate over hot water or in a microwave (see page 11) until melted and smooth. Stir it into the remaining 1 cup of batter.

6. Spoon the chocolate batter over the regular batter in distinct heaping tablespoon "blobs," leaving ½ inch between spoonfuls. Use

49

a skewer or fine knife tip to draw through the globs to marbleize the cake (for more details, see page 184).

7. Place the cheesecake in the larger pan. Carefully pour boiling water around the pan until it comes halfway up the sides of the smaller pan.

8. Put on the middle shelf in the oven and bake for 1 hour until the edges are firm and the top is dull. The center should not shake when the pan is moved. If in doubt, err on the undercooked side as the cake will taste better if it is a little creamier, rather than a little drier. Turn off the oven, open the oven door, and let the cheesecake cool in the oven, in the *bain marie*, for 1 hour. Remove from the oven and *bain marie* and cool completely. Refrigerate overnight.

9. Use a small knife or spatula to free the short ends of the cheesecake. Lift the cheesecake by the extended foil and set it on a cutting board. To cut, use a long nonserrated knife. If the edges are not straight, cut ¼ inch off the edges. Along the long side, measure off 2-inch segments. Cut through the cake and then wiggle the knife side to side to separate the pieces and make room for the knife to come out without marring the surface of the cheesecake. Wipe the blade with a warm, damp cloth after each cut. You will now have strips that are 2 inches wide and 8½ inches long. The last strip will only be 1½ inches wide. It can be set aside or cut into 1½-inch squares. Cut the other strips into 2-inch squares.

Can Prepare Ahead

REFRIGERATED, 3 DAYS; FROZEN, 3 MONTHS

Makes twenty 2-inch squares

6

Pastry Crusts

*P*astry for Passover will amaze and delight your guests. Crumb crusts, standard short pastry crusts, nut crusts, and streusel are no longer forbidden foods. In fact, the crumb crusts are so delicious, you may never use graham cracker crumbs again!

COOKIE CRUMB CRUSTS   52

"GRAHAM CRACKER" CRUST   53

NUT CRUMB CRUST   55

SWEET PASTRY CRUST   56

CRISP MERINGUE DISKS AND TART SHELLS   59

STREUSEL TOPPING   61

51

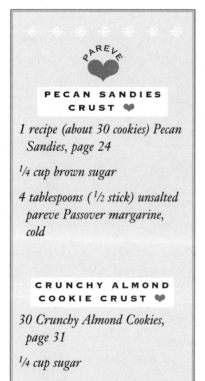

PECAN SANDIES CRUST ♥

1 recipe (about 30 cookies) Pecan Sandies, page 24

¼ cup brown sugar

4 tablespoons (½ stick) unsalted pareve Passover margarine, cold

CRUNCHY ALMOND COOKIE CRUST ♥

30 Crunchy Almond Cookies, page 31

¼ cup sugar

6 tablespoons unsalted pareve Passover margarine, cold

Cookie Crumb Crusts

THESE COOKIE CRUMB CRUSTS (AND THE "GRAHAM CRACKER" CRUST THAT FOLLOWS) HAVE SLIGHTLY DIFFERENT TASTES AND TEXTURES BUT CAN BE USED INTERCHANGEABLY ACCORDING TO YOUR OWN PREFERENCES. COOKIE CRUMB CRUSTS WORK BEST WITH FILLINGS THAT ARE "STICKY," OR LIQUID FILLINGS THAT SOLIDIFY WITH BAKING, SUCH AS CHEESECAKES. WITH MOIST FILLINGS THEY TEND TO FALL APART.

1. Place the cookies in a processor and pulse until finely ground. Measure out 4 cups and save the remainder for another use.

2. Place the ground cookies and sugar in the processor and pulse to blend. Add the margarine or butter and pulse until the dough starts to clump together.

3. Press the crumbs into the bottom of a 9 × 13-inch pan or on the bottom and up the sides of a 9- or 10-inch tube pan.

Place on the middle shelf in the oven and bake at 350°F for 10 minutes, or according to recipe directions. Cool before filling.

Can Prepare Ahead

Unbaked mixture: REFRIGERATED, 1 WEEK; FROZEN, 3 MONTHS

Baked crust: REFRIGERATED, 2 DAYS

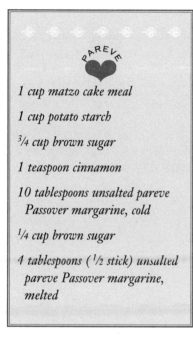

1 cup matzo cake meal

1 cup potato starch

3/4 cup brown sugar

1 teaspoon cinnamon

10 tablespoons unsalted pareve
Passover margarine, cold

1/4 cup brown sugar

4 tablespoons (1/2 stick) unsalted
pareve Passover margarine,
melted

"Graham Cracker" Crust

USE THIS MOCK GRAHAM CRACKER CRUST THE SAME WAY YOU'D USE A REAL GRAHAM CRACKER CRUST. STICKY FILLINGS THAT WILL HOLD THE CRUMBS IN PLACE WORK WELL, AS DO CHOCOLATE OR CHEESE FILLINGS. BE WARNED: THE CRUMBS TASTE SO GOOD, THEY MAY NEVER MAKE IT TO THE PROCESSOR!

1. Preheat oven to 350°F. Line two baking sheets with parchment paper.

2. Place the matzo cake meal, potato starch, brown sugar, and cinnamon in a processor bowl with the metal blade. Pulse on and off until ingredients are blended. Add the margarine and process just until it has been incorporated into the dry ingredients. Turn out onto the parchment paper.

3. Press the mixture together to form pea-sized lumps. Place the baking sheets on the middle and lower racks in the oven. Bake 13 to 15 minutes or until lightly browned, switching the position of the two sheets after 6 minutes. Let cool.

4. Place the lumps in a food processor and pulse until finely ground. Remove from the processor, measure out 4 cups, and save the remainder for another use.

5. Place the 4 cups of ground crumbs and the brown sugar into the processor and pulse to blend. Add the melted butter and pulse until the dough starts to clump together.

6. Press the crumbs into the bottom of a 9 × 13-inch pan or on the bottom and up the sides of a 9- or 10-inch tube pan. Place on the middle shelf in the oven and bake at 350°F for 10 minutes, or according to recipe directions. Cool before filling.

Can Prepare Ahead

——

Unbaked crust mixture: REFRIGERATED, 1 WEEK; FROZEN, 3 MONTHS

Baked crust: REFRIGERATED, 2 DAYS

Makes one 9 × 13-inch crust or one 9- or 10-inch tube pan crust

Nut Crumb Crust

USE INSTEAD OF A COOKIE CRUST WHEN YOUR TIME IS LIMITED.

PAREVE

4 cups unsalted pecan pieces

$1/2$ cup sugar

$1/2$ cup unsalted pareve Passover margarine

VARIATION

Substitute any nuts of your choice.

1. Toast the nuts in a 350°F oven until they are fragrant, 5 to 10 minutes. Put them in the freezer for 5 to 10 minutes just to cool them.

2. Process the sugar in a food processor until it is finely ground. Add the pecans and pulse chop the nuts until they are finely ground. Add the margarine or butter and pulse until well mixed and the crumbs can be pressed together.

3. Press the crumbs into the bottom of a 9 × 13-inch pan or on the bottom and up the sides of a 9 or 10-inch tube pan. Place on the middle shelf in the oven and bake at 350°F for 10 minutes, or according to recipe. Cool before filling.

Can Prepare Ahead

Unbaked crust mixture: REFRIGERATED, 2 WEEKS; FROZEN, 3 MONTHS

Baked crust: REFRIGERATED, 2 MONTHS

Makes one 9 × 13-inch crust or one 9- or 10-inch tube pan crust

55

Sweet Pastry Crust

PAREVE

2 cups matzo cake meal

⅔ cup vanilla sugar, or substitute, page 18

10 tablespoons unsalted pareve Passover margarine, cold, and cut into tablespoon-size pieces

2 large egg yolks

2 to 4 tablespoons water

GLAZE

1 large egg white, whisked with 1 tablespoon water

1. Place the matzo cake meal and the sugar in a processor bowl and process until mixture is well blended. Place the margarine on top of the flour/sugar mix and pulse processor on and off until the margarine is cut into pea-size pieces.

2. Combine the egg yolks and 2 tablespoons water (and extract if using). With the machine running, pour the eggs through the feed tube and process 10 seconds. The dough will not form a ball, but should start to clump together. Feel the dough. It should be neither sticky nor crumbly. If necessary, add 1 teaspoon of water at a time, pulsing 10 seconds and feeling the dough until it is right.

3. Turn out onto a piece of waxed paper and push the dough together. Wrap in plastic wrap and refrigerate for 15 minutes. Roll the dough between wax paper to a thickness of ⅛ inch.

FOR LARGE TARTS

4. Grease the bottom and the fluted sides of a 9- or 10-inch metal tart pan with removable bottom. Remove the top piece of paper and using the bottom piece to hold the dough, flip it onto the tart pan. Do not be alarmed if the dough cracks and the sides fall off. Press the dough down into the tart pan and repair any tears and the sides by pressing the extra dough where necessary.

5. Prick the bottom several times with a fork. Place the pan in the freezer for ½ hour (or up to 3 months ahead). Continue with your chosen recipe, or follow the instructions below if making a shell for another purpose.

6. Preheat the oven to 375°F. Place the tart on a cookie sheet and put in the middle of the oven to bake for 10 to 15 minutes. The tart shell should just be starting to brown. Brush the bottom and the sides with the egg white glaze and continue baking for 3 to 10 minutes. For partially baked shells, the shell should not yet be golden brown. For fully baked shells, the shell should be nicely browned. Remove the tart from the oven and place on a wire rack until completely cooled.

7. To remove the outside of the pan, carefully push up from the center of the bottom. If the sides seem to be sticking anywhere, use a sharp knife to gently loosen and then continue as above. Because the crust is very delicate, it should be filled first and then the rim can be removed.

FOR MINI-TARTS ❤

The easiest pan to use for making mini-tarts is a "Pixie-Bun Pan," which makes 12 round-bottom cupcakes or tarts. The rounded bottom makes it easier for the dough to go in and come out. A pan with 1³/₄-inch holes (available from The Home Economist, source 10, page 198) makes a nice size tart. Small individual tart pans can also be used, as well as mini muffin tins. Any pan used should be well greased.

4. Use a round or fluted 2-inch cookie cutter to cut out dough. Press the circles lightly into the pan. Repair any cracks by pressing dough together, or by adding extra dough, if necessary. Prick the bottoms several times with a fork. Freeze for 15 minutes.

5. Place on the middle shelf in the oven and bake tarts for 10 minutes. Use a feather pastry brush to brush the inside of each tart with the glaze. This will not only seal the tarts, but will also push

down any bubbles that may have formed. Bake for an additional 3 to 5 minutes, or until nicely browned. Place the trays on wire racks and let cool.

6. To remove the tarts from the pan, turn the pan upside down, bend it slightly backward and gently tap to dislodge tarts. Place a clean towel on the table to cushion the tarts as they fall out of the pan; keep the pan close to the towel so the tarts do not have far to fall.

Can Prepare Ahead

Baked, unfilled shells: REFRIGERATED, 1 WEEK; FROZEN, 3 MONTHS

To freeze, place shells unstacked on a cookie sheet and freeze for 1 hour. (The baked shells are too fragile to stack without freezing first.) Tarts may then be stacked with waxed paper between the layers in an airtight storage container. Frozen tarts can be filled frozen. They will defrost in less than 10 minutes.

Makes 54 mini-tarts

Crisp Meringue Disks and Tart Shells

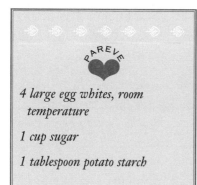

4 large egg whites, room temperature

1 cup sugar

1 tablespoon potato starch

DO NOT MAKE MERINGUES ON HUMID DAYS.

1. Preheat oven to 200°F. Cut two pieces of parchment paper to fit two cookie sheets. Turn the parchment paper so that the curling side is up.

FOR LARGE DISKS: Trace an 8- or 9-inch circle on each piece of parchment.

FOR INDIVIDUAL TARTS: Trace six 3½-inch circles on parchment.

FOR MINI-TARTS: Trace fifteen to twenty 1½-inch circles on each piece of parchment.

Turn the parchment over so that the marked side is facing down and will not be in contact with the food.

2. Place the sugar and potato starch in a processor and process until the sugar is fine and powdery.

3. Place the egg whites in a clean, dry mixer bowl and beat with an electric mixer, on medium speed, until soft peaks form (see "Egg Whites," page 13). Continue beating on medium as you gradually add the sugar. Increase the speed to high and beat until the whites are very thick and marshmallowy.

4. Place a coupler into a large (16-inch) pastry bag and attach a ½-inch plain tip. Fill the bag with the meringue (see piping tips, page 180).

59

5. Holding the bag straight up about ⅛ inch from the cookie sheet, pipe a spiral starting in the center of a circle and continuing to its outside edge. Repeat with the remaining circles.

6. Use your finger dipped into potato starch to smooth down any peaks that occur when you lift the pastry bag off of the circle.

FOR TART SHELLS

7. Make the base using the directions above, then change the tip to a large star tip. The shell can be made by piping a line on top of the outside edge of each circle or by piping rosettes on top of the outside edge. Alternatively, if you feel unable to use a pastry bag, spoon mounds onto each drawn circle and hollow out the centers using a large melon baller.

Place on the middle shelf in the oven and bake for 2 hours. Turn oven off, and leave the meringues in the oven overnight.

Can Prepare Ahead

Unbaked crust mixture: REFRIGERATED, 1 WEEK; FROZEN, 1 MONTH

Store the meringues in an airtight container.

Makes 2 large disks, six 3½-inch tarts, or 50 mini-shells

Streusel Topping

1 cup matzo cake meal

1 cup potato starch

³/4 cup brown sugar

1 teaspoon cinnamon

10 tablespoons unsalted pareve Passover margarine, cold

1. Preheat oven to 350°F. Line two baking sheets with parchment paper.

2. Place the matzo cake meal, potato starch, brown sugar, and cinnamon in a processor bowl with the metal blade. Pulse on and off until ingredients are combined. Add the margarine and process just until it has been blended into the dry ingredients. The dough should be slightly dry. Turn out onto the parchment-lined baking sheets. Press the mixture together to form pea-sized lumps

3. Place the baking sheets on the middle shelf in the oven and bake for 13 to 15 minutes or until lightly browned, switching the position of the two sheets after 6 minutes. Let cool before storing.

Can Prepare Ahead

Unbaked crumbs: REFRIGERATED, 1 WEEK; FROZEN, 3 MONTHS

Baked crumbs: REFRIGERATED, 1 WEEK; FROZEN, 3 MONTHS

Baked, frozen crumbs do not need to be defrosted.

Makes enough for a 9 × 13-inch pan

61

7

Pastries

If you love pastries, you needn't give them up for Passover. Whether you like light and refreshing pastries or sinfully decadent ones, they can be made completely kosher for Passover.

PECAN CARAMEL TART   63

RED AND BLUE NUT TART   66

APPLE TANGERINE CRISP   68

PEAR PINEAPPLE COBBLER   70

ASSORTED MINI-TARTS   72

BROWNED BUTTER STRAWBERRY TART   74

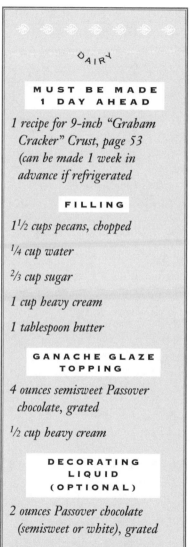

**MUST BE MADE
1 DAY AHEAD**

1 recipe for 9-inch "Graham Cracker" Crust, page 53 (can be made 1 week in advance if refrigerated

FILLING

1½ cups pecans, chopped

¼ cup water

⅔ cup sugar

1 cup heavy cream

1 tablespoon butter

GANACHE GLAZE TOPPING

4 ounces semisweet Passover chocolate, grated

½ cup heavy cream

DECORATING LIQUID (OPTIONAL)

2 ounces Passover chocolate (semisweet or white), grated

1 teaspoon mild vegetable oil

Pecan Caramel Tart

ONE OF MY PERSONAL FAVORITES, THIS TART, WITH A HERRINGBONE BLENDED DESIGN, IS FEATURED ON THE COVER. IT WILL PLEASE THOSE WHO LOVE SWEET, RICH, CHOCOLATE CANDY–LIKE DESSERTS.

1. Preheat oven to 400°F. Grease a 9-inch tart pan. Pack the crumbs into the bottom and up the sides of the pan. Sprinkle the nuts over the crust. Set on a cookie sheet.

2. For the filling, combine the water and sugar in a medium saucepan and heat over medium heat, stirring often, until the sugar is dissolved. Once the liquid begins to boil, do not stir. Heat until the sugar turns a medium amber color, about 10 to 15 minutes.

3. Remove from the heat, tip the pan away from you, and add the cream and the butter. The caramel will lump up. Return to medium heat and cook, stirring constantly, until the caramel lump dissolves and the filling is smooth.

4. Pour the filling over the pecans. Cover with aluminum foil. Bake 40 minutes. Place on a cooling rack, remove the foil, and let cool. Refrigerate overnight. Excess butter will be absorbed into the tart by the morning.

GANACHE TOPPING

5. Place the chocolate in a small bowl. Bring the cream to a boil and pour it over the chocolate. Stir to moisten all of the chocolate. Cover and let stand for 5 minutes.

6. Stir the ganache until melted and mostly smooth (ganache can be made 1 week ahead if refrigerated. To use, it must be liquefied again. To do this, place it in the microwave and heat on medium power until melted, or transfer ganache to the top of a double boiler and heat over warm, but not simmering, water until melted).

Strain the ganache through a fine mesh strainer into another bowl. If not making the optional design, pour the ganache into the center of the tart and let it flow to the edges. Refrigerate for several hours to firm the ganache.

DECORATING

7. If using the decoration, make the decorating liquid by combining the chocolate and oil in a microwave-safe container. Heat for 30 to 60 seconds or until the chocolate is shiny. Stir and continue to heat in 10 second bursts until the chocolate is melted, stirring until smooth. Pour into a pastry bag with a very small plain tip attached. Place it near the tart along with a skewer or knife with a very fine point. To test the thickness of the decorating chocolate, spoon a tablespoon of ganache onto a plate. Pipe a line or two of the decorating chocolate across the ganache. Draw a thin-bladed knife through the piping. If the chocolates blend, the liquid is right. Add more oil if necessary to make the chocolates blend.

8. Blended decorations are made on wet glazes. Therefore, do not pour the ganache on top of the tart until you have read all decorating instructions, have the pastry bag with the decorating liquid by the tart, and have all decorating utensils nearby. Use any of the blended designs described on pages 184–87. After decorating, refrigerate for several hours to firm the ganache and the decorations.

9. Remove from the refrigerator 15 minutes before serving.

10. Because this tart is exceptionally rich, it should be cut into small wedges.

Can Prepare Ahead

———

Ganache: REFRIGERATED, 1 WEEK;
FROZEN, 3 MONTHS

Finished tart: REFRIGERATED, 3 DAYS

———————————

Makes 8 to 10 servings

Red and Blue Nut Tart

CRUST

1 recipe Sweet Pastry Crust,
page 56, prepared in a 9-inch
tart pan, unbaked and chilled
(can be prepared 1 day ahead or
frozen for up to 3 months)

1 large egg white, whisked with
1 tablespoon water

FILLING

66

½ cup sliced almonds

½ cup chopped pecans

¼ cup sugar

5 tablespoons unsalted pareve
Passover margarine, room
temperature

1 large egg yolk, room
temperature

1 large egg, room temperature

1 teaspoon water

1 tablespoon matzo cake meal

1. Preheat oven to 375°F. Place the cold tart shell on a baking sheet. Set it on the center rack of the oven and bake for 15 minutes. Brush with egg white glaze and bake for another 5 to 10 minutes until the glaze is set and the tart has started to brown.

2. While the tart shell is baking, prepare the filling. Place all of the ingredients in a food processor bowl and pulse until the nuts are ground, and all ingredients are well blended. Scrape bowl and pulse a few times to combine.

3. Spread the filling into the baked tart shell, return it to the oven and bake for 5 to 7 minutes until the filling is just barely set.

4. Place the baking sheet on a wire rack until completely cool. Can be done 8 hours ahead.

ASSEMBLY

5. Brush the top of the filling with the wine. Make the glaze by combining the jelly and wine in a small saucepan, and heating until melted and smooth.

Start in the center of the tart with a single berry. Working outward from the center, arrange the berries in alternating circles of raspberries and blueberries.

6. Brush the berries with the glaze, remove the pan rim, and serve. To help prevent the crust from breaking off during cutting, place a finger on the outside crust of the piece being cut to counteract the force of the knife.

TOPPING

1 tablespoon blackberry Passover wine

1 pint fresh raspberries

1 pint fresh blueberries

GLAZE

¼ cup red currant jelly

2 teaspoons blackberry Passover wine

Can Prepare Ahead

Baked, filled tart: REFRIGERATED, 8 HOURS

Finished tart with topping: REFRIGERATED, 3 HOURS

Makes 6 to 8 servings

VARIATION

Any fruit can be used on this filling—pears are especially nice.

A delicious dairy variation is to spoon Crème Patissière, page 151, onto the nut layer and then to top with the berries.

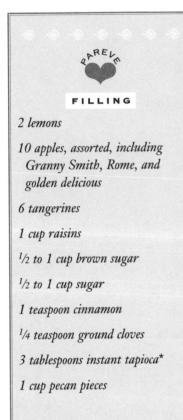

PAREVE

FILLING

2 lemons

10 apples, assorted, including
   Granny Smith, Rome, and
   golden delicious

6 tangerines

1 cup raisins

½ to 1 cup brown sugar

½ to 1 cup sugar

1 teaspoon cinnamon

¼ teaspoon ground cloves

3 tablespoons instant tapioca*

1 cup pecan pieces

TOPPING

1 recipe Streusel Topping, page
   61, baked (unbaked crumbs can
   be made 1 week in advance and
   baked crumbs can be stored for
   2 days at room temperature)

68

Apple Tangerine Crisp

IF YOU LIKE A TARTER DESSERT, USE MORE OF THE
GRANNY SMITHS. INCLUDE A COUPLE OF THE OTHER
APPLES TO VARY THE TEXTURE. FOR A SWEETER FLAVOR,
USE ONLY A COUPLE OF THE GRANNY SMITHS.

1. Preheat oven to 350°F.

2. Squeeze 1 lemon into a large bowl of water. Peel and core the
apples and drop them into the bowl of acidulated water. Cut half of
the apples into 1-inch chunks and place back in the bowl of water.
Grate the remaining apples in a food processor or with a box
grater. Drain the apple chunks, add the grated apple, and squeeze
on the remaining lemon juice.

3. Slice 3 of the tangerines in half. Squeeze and reserve ½ cup
juice. Peel the remaining 3 tangerines. Separate into sections and
cut into 1-inch pieces. Remove seeds.

4. The amount of sugar to use is a matter of personal preference.
Use the smaller quantities for a less sweet and more tart flavor. Add
the sugar and the remaining filling ingredients along with the
reserved juice.

*Note: Without a crust, the crisp doesn't need a thickener, but
if you like a thicker filling, use the tapioca (not certified Kosher
for Passover).

5. Transfer to a buttered 9 × 12-inch pan, or to individual
ramekins. Cover loosely with foil and bake for 1 hour or until the
apples are tender. Remove from the oven.

**GARNISH
(OPTIONAL)**

*1 to 2 cups Meringue Butter-
cream, vanilla, made with
2 sticks margarine, page 131*

VARIATIONS

Pear Pineapple: See page 70

*Pear Vanilla: Substitute pears for
apples and cut into chunks. Delete
tangerines, brown sugar, spices, and
nuts. Use 1½ cups vanilla sugar
(page 17). Dot top with butter, bake,
and top with crumbs.*

*Plain Apple: Delete tangerine and
nuts. Dot top with 3 tablespoons
butter or pareve Passover margarine. Bake just until apples are
barely tender, about 45 minutes. Top
with crumbs.*

*Rhubarb: Use apples or pears and
2 cups rhubarb cut into 1-inch
chunks.*

6. Take off the foil and sprinkle the fruit with the streusel crumbs.
Cool to just warm and serve with the soft buttercream or, for a
dairy dessert, with whipped cream.

Can Prepare Ahead

Baked fruit: REFRIGERATED, 3 DAYS

Finished crisp: REFRIGERATED, 5 HOURS

*If the fruit has been baked ahead, rewarm, covered, in a 350°F oven (about 20
minutes) or in a microwave and then add the crumbs. It also tastes great eaten
at room temperature or cold.*

Makes 8 to 10 servings

69

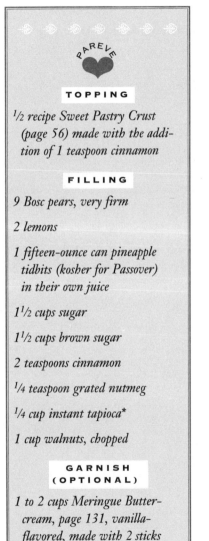

TOPPING

½ recipe Sweet Pastry Crust (page 56) made with the addition of 1 teaspoon cinnamon

FILLING

9 Bosc pears, very firm

2 lemons

1 fifteen-ounce can pineapple tidbits (kosher for Passover) in their own juice

1½ cups sugar

1½ cups brown sugar

2 teaspoons cinnamon

¼ teaspoon grated nutmeg

¼ cup instant tapioca*

1 cup walnuts, chopped

GARNISH (OPTIONAL)

1 to 2 cups Meringue Buttercream, page 131, vanilla-flavored, made with 2 sticks margarine

Pear Pineapple Cobbler

THIS IS NOT A TRUE COBBLER, BECAUSE THE PASTRY ON TOP IS NOT MADE WITH A BISCUIT DOUGH. WHATEVER YOU CHOOSE TO CALL IT, YOU'LL FIND THE FLAVORS OF PEAR, PINEAPPLE, CINNAMON, AND NUTMEG A LITTLE UNUSUAL.

1. Preheat oven to 350°F. Line a cookie sheet with parchment paper.

2. Make the pastry according to the directions. Roll dough to ⅛ inch. Using a 2½-inch daisy or round cookie cutter, cut out 12 daisies. Place on the parchment paper, leaving a small amount of space between each cookie. Put on the middle shelf in the oven and bake the pastry for 12 to 15 minutes until lightly browned. Set on a rack to cool.

3. Peel and core the pears. Squeeze 1 lemon into a container of water and place the pears in the water as you peel them. Grate 5 pears in a processor or with a box grater. Cut the remaining pears into chunks about 1 inch in size. Combine the grated and chunky pears and squeeze the last lemon over them.

4. Reserve ⅜ cup of pineapple juice. Drain the pineapple and add to the pears along with the reserved pineapple juice. Add the sugars, cinnamon, nutmeg, tapioca, and walnuts and place in a greased 9 × 12-inch decorative baking dish. Cover loosely with aluminum foil and bake for 1 hour. (The pears should still be firm.)

*Note: Without a crust, the cobbler doesn't need a thickener, but if you like a thicker filling, use the tapioca (not certified Kosher for Passover).

5. Remove from the oven. Take off the foil and place the daisies over the top. Cool to just warm and serve with the cold, soft buttercream (if making a dairy dessert, serve with Whipped Cream, page 147).

Can Prepare Ahead

———

Sweet pastry: ROOM TEMPERATURE, 2 DAYS; FROZEN, 3 MONTHS

Baked fruit: REFRIGERATED, 2 DAYS

Topped cobbler: REFRIGERATED, 3 HOURS

If the fruit has been made ahead, rewarm in a 350°F oven or in the microwave. Add the cookies and serve warm.

———————————

Makes 8 to 10 servings

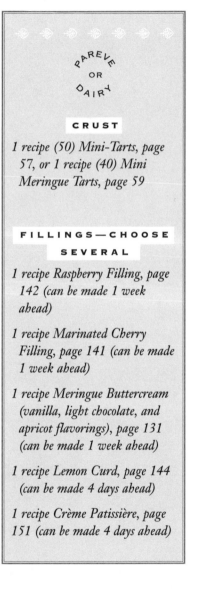

CRUST

1 recipe (50) Mini-Tarts, page 57, or 1 recipe (40) Mini Meringue Tarts, page 59

FILLINGS—CHOOSE SEVERAL

1 recipe Raspberry Filling, page 142 (can be made 1 week ahead)

1 recipe Marinated Cherry Filling, page 141 (can be made 1 week ahead)

1 recipe Meringue Buttercream (vanilla, light chocolate, and apricot flavorings), page 131 (can be made 1 week ahead)

1 recipe Lemon Curd, page 144 (can be made 4 days ahead)

1 recipe Crème Patissière, page 151 (can be made 4 days ahead)

Assorted Mini-Tarts

SERVE MINI-TARTS AS AN ACCOMPANIMENT OR AS PART OF A BUFFET TABLE OF DESSERTS. IF SERVING JUST TARTS, CHOOSE THE LARGER 3½-INCH SIZE. FOR A PLATTER OF MINI-TARTS, USE SEVERAL OF THE FILLING COMBINATIONS TO PROVIDE FOR A VARIETY IN COLOR, TEXTURE AND TASTE. BE WARNED—IF YOU MAKE THREE DIFFERENT KINDS OF TARTS, EVERYONE WILL WANT TO TASTE ONE OF EACH AND GO BACK FOR SECONDS.

**FILLING COMBINATIONS—
1 TEASPOON FILLING PER TART**

♥ Raspberry Vanilla: Use lightly thickened Raspberry Filling and Meringue Buttercream, vanilla flavored. Fill shell ⅔ full with the raspberry sauce and pipe a swirl of buttercream rising out of the shell using a medium star tip (for piping details, see page 180). Top with a fresh raspberry. One half pint of raspberries has about 90 raspberries.

Lemon Curd and Blueberry: Spoon in the Lemon Curd to just below the rim of the tart. Top with 1 to 4 blueberries. There are 75 blueberries to ½ pint.

♥ Chocolate Cherry: Use a medium star tip to pipe light chocolate flavored Meringue Buttercream to just below the rim of the shell. Top with 1 teaspoon of lightly thickened Cherry Filling.

Custard and Fresh Fruit: Brush the inside of the shell with melted chocolate and let harden before filling. Fill with 1 teaspoon Crème

Patissière. Top with fresh raspberries, blueberries, mandarin oranges, pears or minipear flowers (page 171), strawberries, etc. Glaze with fruit glaze (page 191), using the appropriate color.

❤ Chocolate Apricot: Brush the inside of the shell with melted chocolate and let harden. Fill with apricot-flavored Meringue Buttercream (you will need Apricot Filling, page 145, to make this variation). Mix 1 ounce chocolate chips with 1 teaspoon oil and melt in microwave on medium. Drizzle the chocolate over the buttercream in a decorative pattern.

Can Prepare Ahead

Filled tarts: REFRIGERATED, 4 HOURS; ROOM TEMPERATURE, 2 HOURS

DAIRY

FILLING

4 tablespoons (¹⁄₂ stick) unsalted butter

2 large eggs, room temperature

³⁄₄ cup sugar

2 tablespoons matzo cake meal

2 tablespoons potato starch

CRUST

1 recipe Sweet Pastry Crust, made with butter, page 56, prepared in a 9-inch tart pan, chilled and unbaked (can be made 1 day in advance)

TOPPING

3 cups fresh strawberries

¹⁄₄ cup currant jelly

1 tablespoon blackberry Passover wine

Browned Butter Strawberry Tart

BUTTER IS AN ESSENTIAL FLAVORING IN THIS FILLING AND, THEREFORE, MARGARINE SHOULD NOT BE USED AS A SUBSTITUTE. THE FILLING BAKES UP INTO A CAKE-LIKE LAYER THAT MAKES A NICE CONTRAST TO THE CRUNCHY CRUST ON THE BOTTOM AND THE JUICY BERRIES ON THE TOP.

1. Preheat oven to 450°F.

2. Place the butter in a small saucepan. Heat over high heat for a couple of minutes, stirring, until the butter is very fragrant and amber colored. Remove from the heat. When the foam subsides, check the color. If necessary, reheat for a couple of seconds more. Strain, and set aside to cool.

3. Whisk the eggs, gradually adding the sugar. Stir in the matzo cake meal, potato starch, and the cooled browned butter.

4. Pour the filling into the crust, place on a cookie sheet, and put on the middle shelf in the oven. Bake for 5 minutes, reduce temperature to 325°F, and continue to bake until firm, about 40 to 50 minutes. This can be prepared up to 8 hours ahead of time. Do not remove rim, and store at room temperature.

5. Up to 3 hours before serving, arrange the berries using one of the techniques listed on pages 195–96. Heat the jelly with the wine until it is melted and brush over the berries. The rim should be removed just before serving the tart. When cutting through the tart

edge, place a finger on the back of it as counterpressure, otherwise the knife may crack off the edge.

Can Prepare Ahead

Baked, filled tart: REFRIGERATED, 8 HOURS

Finished tart: REFRIGERATED, 3 HOURS

Makes 6 to 8 servings

8

Foundation Cakes

These basic, unadorned cakes form the foundation for many of the recipes included in this book. They are excellent served alone, with simple accompaniments, or used in your own creations.

Before beginning any of these recipes, be sure to read the section on eggs in Chapter 3.

PASSOVER GÉNOISE   77

CHOCOLATE PECAN CAKE   79

ALMOND SPONGE CAKE   81

LADYFINGERS   83

SPONGY BASE LAYER   85

COCOA CAKE ROLL   86

Passover Génoise

GÉNOISE IS A WONDERFUL CAKE RAISED ONLY BY AIR
WHIPPED INTO EGGS. WHEN MOISTENED WITH SUGAR
SYRUP, GÉNOISE BECOMES RICH, VELVETY, AND
DELICIOUS. ALTHOUGH PASSOVER GÉNOISE ABSORBS
FLUID DIFFERENTLY FROM GÉNOISE MADE WITH FLOUR
AND IS NOT AS LIGHT, IT STILL IS AN EXCELLENT
PASSOVER CAKE.

USE GÉNOISE WITH STRAWBERRY BROWN SUGAR CAKE,
PAGE 104, CHOCOLATE MOUSSE CAKE, PAGE 106, AND
HAZELNUT CUSTARD CAKE, PAGE 118, OR WITH ANY OF
THE FILLINGS AND FROSTINGS INCLUDED. DON'T FORGET
TO MOISTEN GÉNOISE WITH ½ TO 1 CUP OF SYRUP
(DEPENDING ON THE MOISTNESS OF YOUR FILLING),
EXCEPT IF USING EXTREMELY MOIST FILLINGS, SUCH AS
STRAWBERRY FILLING.

PAREVE

7 large eggs

1 cup vanilla sugar or substitute,
page 18

½ cup matzo cake meal

½ cup potato starch

¼ cup Passover oil (any kind
except olive oil)

VARIATION

*Nut génoise can be made by process-
ing ⅓ cup of nuts with 1 tablespoon
of the matzo cake meal/potato starch
mixture. Gently fold in the nuts just
before adding the oil. (Nut oil is a
wonderful choice.)*

77

1. Preheat oven to 375°F. Grease pans and line with parchment
paper.

2. Bring about 2 inches of water to a boil in the bottom of a double
boiler. Reduce heat so water is simmering. Place eggs in the top of
a double boiler or in a metal mixer bowl. With a wire whisk, lightly
whisk eggs. Gradually whisk in the sugar (don't add vanilla extract,
if using). Place the eggs over the water and whisk until the eggs are
warm (about 110°F). You can use an instant-read thermometer, or
stick your finger into the eggs. They should feel quite warm, but
not hot.

3. Remove from heat and beat the eggs with an electric mixer, on
high, until they have tripled in volume and are very thick.

4. Sift together the matzo cake meal and the potato starch. Then sift ⅓ of it over the eggs. Fold together with a slotted spoon or rubber scraper. Repeat twice more.

5. Place the oil in a medium microwavable bowl. Microwave for 30 seconds on medium or until the oil is warm. Add the vanilla extract, if using.

6. Stir 2 cups of batter into the oil until blended. Fold this gently into the remaining batter. Pour the batter into the pans. If necessary, carefully spread it to the edges of the pans. Do not tap the pans to remove bubbles.

7. Place on the middle shelf in the oven and bake cakes until lightly browned and springy, according to the following table:

NUMBER	SIZE	TIME
3	8-inch round pans	10–12 minutes
2	8-inch rounds	13–15 minutes
2	10-inch round pans	12–15 minutes
1	12 × 15-inch rectangle	15–20 minutes
2	10 × 15-inch jelly roll pans	8–10 minutes

After the cakes come from the oven, cool them in the pans on wire racks. When cool, invert the cakes onto cake boards. Use another cake board to flip the cakes right side up.

Can Prepare Ahead

———

REFRIGERATED, 2–3 DAYS; FROZEN, 3 MONTHS

Chocolate Pecan Cake

THIS CAKE IS USED WITH BLACK FOREST CAKE, PAGE 112, CHOCOLATE NOISETTE LAYER CAKE, PAGE 117, CHOCOLATE STRAWBERRY TORTE, PAGE 96, AND PAREVE CHOCOLATE PEANUT BUTTER CAKE, PAGE 102. IT CAN BE USED WITH ANY FROSTING OR FILLING.

PAREVE

½ cup chopped pecans

¼ cup matzo cake meal

8 ounces pareve Passover semi-sweet chocolate, chopped or chips

½ cup boiling water

8 large eggs, room temperature

1 cup sugar

1. Preheat oven to 350°F. Grease two 9-inch round cake pans and place parchment paper in the bottom of each.

2. Place the pecans and the matzo cake meal in the bowl of a processor. Pulse on and off until the nuts are finely ground. Transfer mixture to a container and reserve. Dust out the processor bowl with a clean towel, but do not wash.

3. Place the chocolate in the food processor bowl and process until finely grated. Add the boiling water and process until the chocolate is melted and smooth (about 5 seconds).

4. In a large mixing bowl beat the eggs just to blend. Gradually beat in the sugar. Increase the speed to high and beat until the eggs are thick, pale, and tripled in volume.

5. Sprinkle half of the matzo-nut mixture over the eggs and gently fold into the eggs. Repeat with the remaining matzo nut mix.

6. Add the chocolate in a stream, folding it in gently, until the batter is brown. Pour batter into the prepared pans. Place on the middle shelf in the oven and bake for 25 to 35 minutes or until a tester comes out with no crumbs attached. Place the pans on a cooling rack. Loosen the sides of the cakes with a small metal spatula and then let them cool in the pans.

7. Place a cake board on each cake and invert pans. Reinvert so that the cakes are right side up. If the cake is to be used in a layer cake, freeze the top cake for 1 hour to make it easier to handle.

Can Prepare Ahead

REFRIGERATED, 1 DAY; FROZEN, 3 MONTHS

If cakes have been frozen, defrost at room temperature 1 hour or overnight in the refrigerator.

Almond Sponge Cake

THIS VERY MOIST CAKE CAN BE EATEN PLAIN, WITH
FRUIT, FRUIT SAUCE, GLAZED, OR WITH ANY LIGHT
TEXTURED FILLING OR FROSTING. WHIPPED CREAM AND
BERRIES ARE AN EXCELLENT ACCOMPANIMENT,
ESPECIALLY WHEN THE CAKE IS FRESHLY MADE.
ANOTHER EXCELLENT COMBINATION IS TO SUBSTITUTE
HAZELNUTS FOR THE ALMONDS, AND THEN GLAZE THE
TORTE (USE HALF RECIPE) WITH GANACHE. RECIPES
USING ALMOND SPONGE CAKE INCLUDE PEACH MELBA
TORTE, PAGE 97, PEAR FLOWER ALMOND TORTES, PAGE
94, AND ALMOND CHERRY LAYER CAKE, PAGE 108.

PAREVE

2½ cups sliced almonds

3 tablespoons matzo cake meal

½ teaspoon cinnamon

8 large eggs, room temperature,
separated

1¼ cups vanilla sugar or
substitute, page 18

1. Preheat oven to 350°F. Grease two 9-inch round cake pans and
line the bottoms with parchment paper.

2. Toast the almonds in the oven for 5 to 10 minutes or until
aromatic. Put the nuts in the freezer for 5 minutes to cool them.

3. Place half of the nuts and 1 tablespoon matzo cake meal in a
processor bowl and process until finely ground. Remove from the
bowl, add the remaining nuts, remaining matzo cake meal, and
the cinnamon, and process until finely ground. Combine with
the first batch.

4. Place the egg yolks in a large mixer bowl and beat with an
electric mixer at medium speed just to blend the eggs together.
Gradually add 1 cup of the sugar and continue beating until the
eggs are thick, pale yellow, and the mixture will hold a ribbon.

5. Fold in the nuts in three additions. In a large, clean, and grease-
free bowl, beat the egg whites until soft peaks form. Gradually add

¼ cup sugar and continue beating until the whites are stiff but not dry. Stir ⅓ of the whites into the yolks to lighten the batter. Fold in the remaining whites until no white streaks show. Divide the batter between the pans.

6. Place on the middle shelf in the oven and bake 25 to 35 minutes or until a tester inserted in the middle of the cake comes out dry.

7. Cool the cakes in the pans set on wire racks. When cool run a knife around the edges and then invert onto cake boards and re-invert onto another set of cake boards so that the cakes are right side up. Press down lightly onto the raised edges. They will spread out toward the sides. Lift off the loosened crust, which will level the cakes. If you want a hollow in the center of the cake, bake in a springform instead, and do not invert (just remove the ring when the cakes are cool).

8. When the cakes are first made they are very moist and fragile. If you are going to place one on top of the other in a layer cake, freeze the top layer for 1 hour so that it is easier to work with. If the cakes are wrapped in foil and left at room temperature overnight, they will firm up and can be handled without freezing.

Can Prepare Ahead

—

REFRIGERATED, 1 DAY; FROZEN, 3 MONTHS

If cakes have been frozen, leave at room temperature for 1 hour to defrost, or refrigerate overnight.

Ladyfingers

LADYFINGERS ARE USED IN PEACH RASPBERRY TIRAMISU, PAGE 123, AND TIRAMISU, PAGE 121. THEY CAN ALSO BE MOISTENED WITH SIMPLE SYRUP, LIGHTLY COATED WITH JELLY OR FROSTING, AND PRESSED TOGETHER TO FORM LOW-FAT COOKIES. IF USED IN OTHER RECIPES, DON'T FORGET TO MOISTEN WITH SYRUP.

PAREVE

1 cup Passover powdered sugar or 1 cup granulated sugar mixed with 1 tablespoon potato starch

6 large eggs, room temperature, separated

¹/₂ cup plus 1 tablespoon vanilla sugar or substitute, divided (see page 18)

³/₈ cup matzo cake meal

³/₈ cup potato starch

VARIATION

Lemon Ladyfingers: Subtract 1 egg and add 3 tablespoons lemon juice.

1. Preheat oven to 400°F. Line two cookie sheets with parchment paper, curl side up. To make 3-inch ladyfingers, use a permanent marker to draw two lines, 3 inches apart from each other. Repeat until the whole sheet is lined, leaving a ¹/₄-inch space between each set of lines. Turn the parchment paper over, so that the curl now faces down, and the lines are facing the baking sheet (never pipe directly onto pencil, pen, or marker lines).

2. If you are not using powdered sugar, place the regular sugar and the potato starch in a food processor and pulse process until the sugar is very fine. The sugar will be grittier than powdered sugar but it will be okay for this recipe. If you have a clean coffee grinder or spice grinder, transfer the processed sugar in small batches and grind until the sugar looks like confectioner's sugar. Set aside.

3. In a large mixer bowl, whisk the egg yolks while gradually adding ¹/₂ cup sugar (add extract, if using). With an electric mixer, beat on high speed until the yolks are pale, thick, and form a ribbon, about 5 minutes.

4. Place the egg whites in a large, clean, grease-free mixer bowl. Using clean, dry beaters, beat on high speed to soft peaks. Add 1 tablespoon of sugar and beat until whites are stiff but not dry.

5. Sift together the matzo cake meal and potato starch. Sift ⅓ of this over the egg yolks and then spoon ⅓ of the egg whites on top of that. Fold gently together. Repeat twice more, gently folding the ingredients together.

6. Place a ½-inch plain tip into a pastry bag and fill the bag with the batter. To pipe ladyfingers that are about 1 to 1¼ inches wide, start with the tip ¼ inch down from one of the lines you have drawn. As the batter comes out it will spread up to the line. Continue squeezing and move the tip downward to the bottom line. Leave ¼ to ½ inch between ladyfingers. Pipe all of the ladyfingers (for piping tips, see page 180).

7. If using powdered sugar, dust the ladyfingers liberally. If using the granulated sugar, sift it through a fine mesh strainer and use sparingly, as it will still be a little gritty.

8. Place sheet on the middle shelf in the oven and bake for 8 to 10 minutes until lightly browned. Let the ladyfingers cool on the parchment paper placed on a wire rack.

9. For Toasted Ladyfingers: Preheat the oven to 200°F. Place on the middle shelf in the oven and bake the cooked ladyfingers for 1 hour or until hard and dry.

Can Prepare Ahead

REFRIGERATED, 1 WEEK; FROZEN, 3 MONTHS

Frozen ladyfingers defrost in about 10 minutes.

Makes 42 ladyfingers or one 9-inch disc and 22 fingers

Spongy Base Layer

SPONGY BASE LAYER IS USED IN ALMOST SEVEN LAYER
CAKE, PAGE 126, AND APRICOT WALNUT PAVÉ, PAGE 110.
IT CAN BE USED IN ANY MULTI-LAYERED CAKE.

PAREVE

10 large eggs, room
temperature, separated

3/4 cup plus 1/3 cup, vanilla
sugar or substitute, divided
(see page 18)

1/2 cup plus 2 tablespoons matzo
cake meal

1/2 cup plus 2 tablespoons potato
starch

SERVING SUGGESTIONS

*Be sure to moisten Spongy Base
Layer with about 1 cup of syrup, or
the cake will be too dry. Preferably,
layer cakes made with a spongy
base should be made at least two
days ahead.*

1. Preheat oven to 400°F. Grease the bottom of two 10 × 15-inch
jelly roll pans. Line the pans with parchment paper. Do not grease
or flour the parchment.

2. In a large mixer bowl, whisk the egg yolks while gradually
adding 3/4 cup of sugar. Using an electric mixer, beat on high speed
until the yolks are pale, thick, and form a ribbon, about 5 minutes.

3. Sift together the matzo cake meal and potato starch. Sift on top
of the egg yolks, but do not stir.

4. Place the whites in a large, clean, grease-free mixer bowl. Using
clean, dry beaters, beat the egg whites on high speed to soft peaks.
Gradually add 1/3 cup sugar and beat until whites are stiff but not dry.

5. Stir 1/3 of the whites into the yolks to lighten the batter. Gently
fold in the remaining whites just until no white streaks remain.

6. Divide the batter between the two pans. Use an offset spatula or
other tool to spread the batter to the edges and level the top.

7. Place on the middle shelf in the oven and bake 10 minutes until
nicely browned and springy. Cool in the pans, on wire racks.

Can Prepare Ahead

REFRIGERATED, 2 DAYS; FROZEN, 3 MONTHS

85

Cocoa Cake Roll

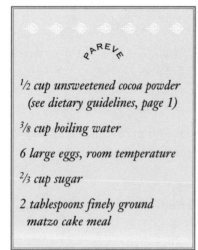

PAREVE

½ cup unsweetened cocoa powder
(see dietary guidelines, page 1)

⅜ cup boiling water

6 large eggs, room temperature

⅔ cup sugar

2 tablespoons finely ground
matzo cake meal

COCOA CAKE ROLL IS USED IN CHOCOLATE BUTTER
PECAN ROLL, PAGE 114. IT ALSO TASTES GREAT WITH
WHIPPED CREAM, NOISETTE FLUFF, OR ANY
BUTTERCREAM.

1. Preheat oven to 350°F. Lightly grease a 9 × 12-inch jelly roll pan. Line with parchment paper leaving a 3-inch overhang on each end. Grease and sprinkle with matzo cake meal.

2. Mix the cocoa and boiling water in a small bowl, and stir until smooth. In a large mixer bowl, beat the eggs to blend, add the sugar, gradually, and then increase speed to medium high (or high on a portable beater). Beat until the eggs are pale in color and very thick (the eggs should form a ribbon, see page 14). Sprinkle the matzo cake meal over the eggs and fold in with a slotted spoon or rubber scraper.

3. Remove 1 cup of eggs and stir into the chocolate. Fold in the remaining eggs using a slotted spoon or a rubber scraper just until the batter is brown.

4. Spoon the batter into the prepared pan. Place on the middle shelf in the oven and bake for 15 minutes or until springy. Remove pan to a cooling rack. Cover with a piece of waxed paper and then a damp towel. Cool completely (can be done up to 2 days ahead, refrigerated—bring cake back to room temperature before filling).

5. When ready to fill, remove the towel and waxed paper. Loosen the long edges by nudging the cake edge with your finger just until it is off the rim of the pan.

6. Using the overhanging parchment paper, lift up the cake and set on a work surface. Fill with desired filling. Lift up one of the short ends by the paper, loosen the edge of the cake, and fold about 1 inch over the filling. Use the paper to roll the cake all the way up. Roll the cake off of the waxed paper and onto a work surface that can be placed in the freezer (such as a cake board or cookie sheet). Decorate as desired, then freeze until firm enough to transfer cake to a serving platter. Freeze or refrigerate as recipe requires.

Can Prepare Ahead

Unrolled cake: REFRIGERATED, 2 DAYS; DO NOT FREEZE

Rolled cake: VARIES WITH TYPE OF FILLING

9

Tortes

In several European languages, the word "torte" (or "torta") simply means cake. *However, many chefs and cookbook authors tend to think of a torte as a special class of cake having little or no flour. Since all Passover desserts are devoid of flour, I have classified tortes as those desserts with a single layer of cake. Whether classically dense, like the Chocolate Fudge Torte, or light and refreshing, like the Peach Melba Torte, all of these recipes make elegant desserts that will please you at any time of the year.*

CHOCOLATE FUDGE TORTE   89

CHOCOLATE RASPBERRY SILK TORTE   91

PEAR FLOWER ALMOND TORTES   94

CHOCOLATE STRAWBERRY TORTE   96

PEACH MELBA TORTE   97

CHOCOLATE PEANUT BUTTER CARAMEL TORTE   99

Chocolate Fudge Torte

CAKE MUST BE PREPARED ONE DAY IN ADVANCE.

PAREVE

20 ounces pareve Passover semi-sweet chocolate, chopped

10 tablespoons unsalted pareve Passover margarine

6 large eggs, room temperature, separated

2 teaspoons matzo cake meal

2 tablespoons sugar

FROSTING

1½ cups Meringue Buttercream, page 131, vanilla flavored, made with 2½ sticks margarine (can be prepared 1 week in advance)

GARNISH

1 cup chocolate shavings, page 187

1. Preheat oven to 425°F. Heat water in a teapot to boiling. Have ready a baking pan large enough to hold a 9-inch round cake pan with space around to hold the boiling water.

2. Grease the bottom of the 9-inch round cake pan. Place a piece of parchment paper in the bottom of the pan and grease the paper with margarine, too.

3. Combine the chocolate and margarine in the top of a double boiler. Melt together, over hot but not simmering water, and stir until smooth. Transfer to a mixer bowl and cool 5 minutes.

4. Using a wire whisk, whisk the egg yolks just to blend. With an electric mixer on low, beat them into the chocolate a little at a time. Beat in the matzo cake meal.

5. Place egg whites in a clean grease-free bowl. Using clean grease-less beaters beat the egg whites on medium speed until soft peaks form. Increase speed to high, gradually add the sugar, and continue beating until the whites are stiff but not dry (see page 13).

6. Stir ⅓ of the whites into the batter and then gently fold in the remaining whites. Transfer to the prepared 9-inch round pan.

7. Place the pan into the larger pan, and pour boiling water around the pan to come ½ way up the sides of the 9-inch pan. Place on the middle shelf of the oven and bake for 25 to 30 minutes until the surface dulls, but the cake still looks uncooked in the center. Remove from oven, place on a wire rack, and cool completely. Refrigerate overnight.

8. To remove the cake from the pan, set a cake board on top of the cake and flip the pan over. Fill a pot with 1 inch of water and heat to boiling. Place the pot on the bottom of the cake pan and rub over the bottom of the pan until the cake drops out. Remove the parchment paper, place another cake board on the cake, and reinvert.

DECORATIONS AND GARNISHES

9. If you wish to decorate the sides of the torte, spread them smoothly with buttercream. Spread a very thin layer of buttercream over the top of the cake. Pipe a shell border (see page 181) around the top edge. Use a spoon to sprinkle chocolate shavings in the center so that none of the topping is visible. The sides can also be covered with chocolate shavings. Serve immediately or store. Let cake sit at room temperature for 15 minutes before serving.

10. Because this cake is messy to cut, it is wise to cut it ahead. Have a pitcher of warm water and a towel handy. Make a cut and rock the knife side to side to make space for its removal. Dip the knife into the warm water, wipe dry, and make the second cut. Make small pieces as the cake is very rich. Repeat with the rest of the torte. Arrange the sections in a circle on a platter, with a small space between each wedge.

Can Prepare Ahead

REFRIGERATED, 2 DAYS; FROZEN, 3 MONTHS

Frozen cake may be defrosted in the refrigerator overnight.
Let stand at room temperature 15 minutes before serving.

Makes 8 to 16 servings

Chocolate Raspberry Silk Torte

PAREVE

16 ounces semisweet Passover chocolate, chopped (or chips)

4 sticks (1 pound) unsalted pareve Passover margarine

1 cup sugar

1 cup Passover blackberry wine

½ cup seedless raspberry jam

8 large eggs, room temperature

Garnishes and sauces (optional)

1 recipe Raspberry Sauce, page 156

1½ pints fresh raspberries

1. Preheat oven to 325°F. Grease a 10-inch round cake pan with margarine. Place a piece of parchment paper on the bottom of the pan. Boil water in a pot or teakettle and set aside. Have ready another baking pan large enough to hold the 10-inch round with space around to hold water (for water bath).

2. Place chocolate in food processor bowl and pulse chop until chocolate is finely grated.

3. Combine margarine, sugar, wine, and jam in a medium saucepan. Heat over medium, stirring occasionally until sugar dissolves and margarine is melted. Increase heat and bring to a boil. Turn the food processor on and pour the hot liquid through the feed tube. Process until the chocolate is melted.

4. Whisk the eggs together. With the processor on, add the eggs through the feed tube and process just to incorporate the egg. Scrape the bowl and pulse a few more times.

5. Pour the batter into the prepared pan. Place in the larger pan and pour the boiling water around it until the water comes halfway up the sides of the round pan (called a *bain marie*).

Place on the middle shelf in the oven and bake for 45 minutes. The surface will still be shiny, but dry to the touch. Remove from the water bath and cool completely on a wire rack.

6. To unmold the cake, place a 9-inch cardboard cake round on top and then invert. The torte should fall out. If it doesn't, heat the bottom of the pan by rubbing a hot teakettle on the pan bottom until the torte falls out. Remove the pan and take the parchment off of the cake.

DECORATIONS AND GARNISHES

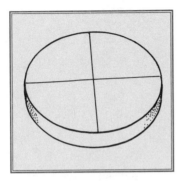

9.1

7. When the parchment is removed from the cake there should be an interesting pattern in the cake. If this is not appealing, smooth the top with a long spatula.

On this smooth surface, a simple striped decoration can be made by marking the cake into quarters using a long knife *(see illustration 9.1)*.

Draw a serrated knife across each quarter so that adjacent quarters are striped perpendicular to each other *(see illustration 9.2)*.

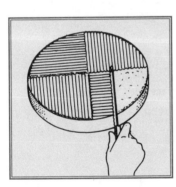

9.2

8. An even easier decoration would be to cover the top of the cake with fresh raspberries. You will need 1½ pints of berries to cover the whole top. For a truly special presentation, serve each slice on a pool of Raspberry Sauce, page 156, or for a dairy dessert, serve with Crème Anglaise, page 160.

9. The cake can be served cold, but will be easier to slice if served at room temperature. To enhance the appearance of each slice, wipe the knife blade off with a damp cloth between cuts (for more details on cutting cakes, see page 189).

Can Prepare Ahead

—

Ungarnished torte: REFRIGERATED, 2 DAYS;
FROZEN, 3 MONTHS

Decorated with fresh berries:
REFRIGERATED, 3 HOURS

*The berries can be kept longer if they are glazed with Fruit Glaze or Stabilized
Fruit Glaze, pages 191–92.*

—

Makes 10 to 16 servings

DAIRY

COMPONENTS

1 recipe (2 layers) Almond
Sponge Cake, page 81, baked
and cooled (can be prepared
1 day in advance)

1 recipe (4 pears) Caramel
Poached Pears, page 167, cold,
some syrup reserved (can be
prepared 2 days in advance)

1 cup Meringue Buttercream,
page 131, see directions at right
(can be prepared 4 days in
advance)

1 recipe Fruit Glaze, page 191,
using apple

SAUCE

1 cup Crème Anglaise, page 160,
or Caramel Pear Cream Sauce,
page 164 (can be prepared 4
days in advance)

Pear Flower Almond Tortes

THE EASIEST WAY TO MAKE A DESSERT WITH SO MANY
COMPONENTS IS TO MAKE SOME, OR ALL, OF THE PARTS
AHEAD OF TIME. THE COMPONENTS CAN BE MADE IN ANY
ORDER USING THE CHART BELOW, BUT TIME CAN BE
SAVED IF THE BUTTERCREAM IS MADE JUST BEFORE
ASSEMBLY, SO IT DOES NOT HAVE TO BE RESOFTENED.

1. Make buttercream with $2\frac{1}{4}$ to $2\frac{1}{2}$ sticks of margarine, using
vanilla, light chocolate, nut, or raspberry flavoring.

2. Use a 4-inch round cookie cutter, glass jar, or other suitable
object to cut out 6 rounds of cake (3 from each layer).

3. Using a medium star tip, pipe a spiral or spread about 2 tablespoons of filling onto each cake round (see chapter 14, "Decorating
Tips"). Cover and store. Can be done 1 day ahead (or frozen).

4. Make 6 Pear Flowers, page 171. You will have 1 extra pear just
in case you make a mistake. If made more than a few hours before
serving, use a feather brush to glaze with the apple fruit glaze.
Store covered in the refrigerator (can be placed directly on cake
and refrigerated or on a plate until cake has been prepared).

5. Place 1 Pear Flower in the center of each cake round. If preparing ahead, also glaze pears with the fruit glaze. Refrigerate until
ready to sauce plates.

DECORATING AND SERVING

6. Marbleizing: Spoon about 2 tablespoons of Crème Anglaise onto
a dessert plate (sauce needs to be at least room temperature or the

glaze will set too fast and you won't be able to swirl the chocolate). Tip the plate so that the sauce covers the entire bottom.

7. For decorating chocolate: Combine chocolate and honey over hot water, or in microwave on medium power for 30 to 60 seconds until shiny, and then in 10-second bursts, stirring after each, until melted and smooth.

8. Place some sauce on a "test" plate and drizzle on some of the chocolate decorating liquid. Use a knife to draw through the chocolate to see if it is thin enough to blend with the sauce. If the chocolate hardens and will not blend, add 1 teaspoon or more of warmed pear liquid or honey, until the chocolate will blend.

9. Pipe or drizzle chocolate in circular loops over the sauced plates. Use a fine-pointed knife or skewer to draw through the loops to swirl the chocolate and sauce together. Refrigerate until cold or serve immediately with a cake round set in the center. For other decorations, see chapter 14.

DECORATING CHOCOLATE

2 ounces Passover chocolate, preferably not chips

1 tablespoon honey

1 teaspoon or more reserved pear liquid

VARIATION

For pareve: Use Raspberry Sauce, page 156, or Pareve Light Chocolate Sauce, page 159.

Can Prepare Ahead

REFRIGERATED, 1 DAY FROZEN;
3 MONTHS WITHOUT PEAR

Frozen cake, with or without frosting, can be defrosted, covered, in the refrigerator overnight, and then topped with pear on the serving dish.

Makes 6 servings

95

Chocolate Strawberry Torte

DAIRY

$^{1}/_{2}$ recipe (9-inch layer)
Chocolate Pecan Cake, page
79, baked and cooled (can be
prepared 1 day in advance)

$^{1}/_{2}$ recipe Strawberry Filling,
page 143; puree the berries
before thickening (can be prepared 2 days in advance)

$^{1}/_{2}$ recipe Ganache Frosting,
page 148 (can be prepared 4
days in advance)

VARIATION

One-half recipe of Raspberry Filling,
page 142, can be used instead of
the strawberry. Pour it while still
slightly warm onto the cake. Cool,
and refrigerate overnight. For
pareve, use Sabayan Chocolate
Frosting, dark, page 135, instead of
the Ganache. You can also use
Whipped Cream (dairy), page 147,
or Vanilla Buttercream (pareve),
page 132, instead of the Ganache.

1. Place the cake on an 8-inch cake board. Spread or pipe frosting on the sides of the torte (and the top, if desired).

2. Using a pastry bag with a medium star tip, pipe a $^{3}/_{8} \times ^{3}/_{8}$-inch line of ganache along the top edge of the cake to hold in the filling. If you cannot pipe all the way around without a break in the line, start the new line with a shell that tips inward toward the center, and then continue the circle. This can be done several times around the circle, and creates a nice design. If desired, pipe a small circle in the center of the cake and one more circle between the outer and inner rings of frosting, using the above method. Freeze for 15 minutes to firm.

3. Place the cake on a serving platter and pipe a line of ganache along the bottom edge of the cake using the above method also, but having the shell facing upward towards the top of the cake. Fill the circles with the filling. Refrigerate or serve.

Can Prepare Ahead

REFRIGERATED, 1 DAY

Makes 6 to 8 servings

Peach Melba Torte

CAKE MUST BE MADE 1 DAY IN ADVANCE.

PAREVE OR DAIRY

½ recipe (one 9-inch layer) Almond Sponge Cake, page 81, baked in a 9-inch round cake pan, cooled (can be prepared 1 day in advance)

½ recipe Raspberry Filling, page 142, made with 5 teaspoons potato starch, warm

1 cup sliced almonds

3 to 4 peaches (freestones), fresh and ripe

2 lemons

1 recipe Fruit Glaze, using apricot jam, page 191

GARNISHES (OPTIONAL)

1 pint raspberries, fresh

1 recipe Whipped Cream (dairy) page 147 or Meringue Buttercream (pareve) page 131 (can be prepared 4 days in advance)

1. For this recipe you need a ¹⁄₁₆-inch hollow in the top of the cake to hold the filling. If necessary, press down on the edges of the cake to lessen the hollow. If the cake is flat, you can build up the edges with almond slices. Dab a small amount of the filling on the bottom of each almond. Place a row of almonds along the perimeter of the cake. Place the second row staggered, just like a brick or stone wall would be built, and continue building the wall until the hollow is even and deep enough to accommodate the filling. Reserve the remaining almonds for garnish.

2. Pour the filling slowly into the hollow to create a thin (¹⁄₁₆-inch) layer of filling (you will need slightly more than half of the filling). Reserve excess filling. Cool completely, and then refrigerate overnight.

3. Loosen the peach skins by plunging peaches into boiling water for 30 seconds. Cool under cold water and peel. Slice peaches into wedges a scant ⅛ inch thick. To prevent darkening, toss the peach wedges in fresh lemon juice.

4. Arrange the peaches over the raspberry filling in overlapping circles. Start from the outside edge with the tips of the peaches perpendicular to cake edge. Continue inward with tips overlapping. For more details, see "Carnation Design," page 193.

5. Brush apricot fruit glaze over peaches. If dessert will not be served within 4 hours, use stabilized fruit glaze. Brush the side of the torte with the fruit glaze, crush the reserved almonds lightly

If freestone peaches are not available, substitute Vanilla Poached Pears, page 169.

and press them to the sides. Instead of the glaze, the peaches can be brushed with some of the extra raspberry filling. It might be necessary to thin it with a little wine.

GARNISHES (OPTIONAL)

6. For pareve: Make pareve, vanilla buttercream using 2 sticks of margarine. Refrigerate until cold. Garnish plates with a dollop of the very soft buttercream (or whipped cream for dairy dessert) and scatter some fresh raspberries on each plate.

Can Prepare Ahead

REFRIGERATED, 3 HOURS, 1 DAY IF USING
STABILIZED GLAZE

Makes 6 to 8 servings

Chocolate Peanut Butter Caramel Torte

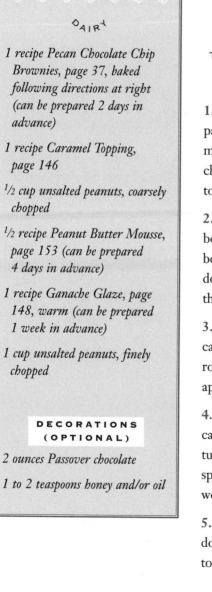

1 recipe Pecan Chocolate Chip Brownies, page 37, baked following directions at right (can be prepared 2 days in advance)

1 recipe Caramel Topping, page 146

1/2 cup unsalted peanuts, coarsely chopped

1/2 recipe Peanut Butter Mousse, page 153 (can be prepared 4 days in advance)

1 recipe Ganache Glaze, page 148, warm (can be prepared 1 week in advance)

1 cup unsalted peanuts, finely chopped

DECORATIONS (OPTIONAL)

2 ounces Passover chocolate

1 to 2 teaspoons honey and/or oil

THIS TORTE WILL CUT AND LOOK BEST WHEN COLD, BUT IS EVEN MORE DELICIOUS AT ROOM TEMPERATURE.

1. Preheat oven to 350°F. Grease a 9-inch round cake pan, place parchment in the bottom, and grease and "flour" the pan with matzo cake meal. Substitute unsalted peanuts for the pecans, and chop the chocolate chips. Bake for 25 to 30 minutes or until a toothpick inserted in the center comes out with a moist crumb.

2. Trim the edges of a 9-inch cake board so that it fits snugly in the bottom of a 9-inch springform pan. Place the cake on the cake board and put it on the bottom plate of the springform. If the cake does not touch the sides of the pan, press down lightly on it so that the cake spreads to meet the pan edges.

3. Make the Caramel Topping, and pour immediately onto the cake. Sprinkle the nuts over the top of the caramel. Let cool to room temperature and then refrigerate until the caramel firms up, approximately 1 hour.

4. Make the Peanut Butter Mousse and spoon on top of the cooled caramel. (If the mousse was made ahead, bring to room temperature, or heat in a microwave on low, stirring until soft enough to spread.) Level the mousse as best as possible (an offset spatula works well). Refrigerate for several hours to firm up the mousse.

5. If the ganache has been made ahead, place it in the top of a double boiler and heat over hot water until it liquefies. If you plan to use the optional decoration, combine the chocolate and honey

99

or oil according to the directions under "Blending Chocolate," page 187. Be sure to test the blending chocolate on the ganache according to those directions.

6. Pour the ganache through a fine mesh strainer onto the top of the mousse to make a ½-inch layer. Reserve and refrigerate the remaining ganache. Make the decoration using the petal, spider-web, or herringbone design on pages 185–87. Let cool to room temperature, and then refrigerate overnight.

7. The next day, run a heated knife around the perimeter of the cake and remove the springform sides. Smooth the edges with a knife or decorating spatula. Soften the ganache in the microwave on low. Heat for 10 seconds, stir, and repeat until the ganache is soft enough to spread. Spread a thin layer of the ganache on the sides of the torte, being careful not to disturb the decoration on the top. Hold the torte in one hand and use the other hand to scoop up a handful of nuts. Pat the nuts onto the sides of the cake by placing the pinkie edge of your hand at the bottom of the torte. Then move upward as you pat on the nuts. In this way the nuts will be preceding you and you won't end up with chocolate all over your hands. Refrigerate until ready to serve.

8. Cut torte with a heated knife and rock it side to side to make room for the knife to come out without marring the surface. Wipe blade off between cuts.

Can Prepare Ahead

REFRIGERATED, 2 DAYS; FROZEN, 3 MONTHS

Makes 10 to 14 servings

10
Layered Cakes

There is no dessert more impressive than a beautifully presented layer cake. These exceptional cakes will bring the highest accolades from family and friends. Don't let the number of components frighten you; all of them can be made ahead. Pace yourself by making one part one day, and another part another day. Prepared in this manner, they are no harder to make than any other cake, and the results will amaze you. For the Seder meal or for a special occasion like a birthday or anniversary nothing delights like a layered cake.

PAREVE CHOCOLATE PEANUT BUTTER CAKE   102

STRAWBERRY BROWN SUGAR CAKE   104

CHOCOLATE MOUSSE CAKE   106

ALMOND CHERRY LAYER CAKE   108

APRICOT WALNUT PAVÉ   110

BLACK FOREST CAKE   112

CHOCOLATE BUTTER PECAN ROLL   114

CHOCOLATE NOISETTE LAYER CAKE   117

HAZELNUT CUSTARD CAKE   118

TIRAMISU   121

PEACH RASPBERRY TIRAMISU   123

ALMOST SEVEN LAYER CAKE   126

Pareve Chocolate Peanut Butter Cake

1 recipe Chocolate Pecan Cake, page 79 (use unsalted peanuts instead of the pecans, and in addition fold in 1/2 cup of chopped unsalted peanuts just before pouring batter into the pans; can be prepared 2 days in advance)

1 recipe each Sabayon Butter Pecan Frosting, page 138, and Chocolate Frosting, page 135, see directions at right (can be prepared 2 days in advance)

102

GARNISH (OPTIONAL)

2 cups dry roasted peanuts coarsely chopped

WHETHER DAIRY AND DENSE LIKE THE PRECEDING RECIPE, OR LIGHT AND PAREVE LIKE THIS ONE, PEANUTS AND CHOCOLATE ARE A WINNING COMBINATION. THANK GOODNESS PEANUTS ARE NOW ACCEPTABLE FOR PASSOVER!

1. Place cake layers on cake boards. Freeze 1 layer for 15 minutes to make it easier to place on top of the frosting.

2. Make the frostings, omitting the chocolate chips from the butter pecan frosting and adding 1 cup unsalted peanut butter and $\frac{1}{2}$ cup chopped unsalted peanuts.

3. Spread the peanut butter frosting thickly over the cake. Remove the other layer from the freezer and place on top of the frosting. Press lightly to level the top. With a cake-decorating spatula remove any oozing filling.

4. Spread the chocolate frosting over the sides and thickly onto the top of the cake. Level the top of the frosting using a long decorating spatula. Draw a serrated cake-decorating tool across the top, remove excess frosting from the perimeter, and then coat the sides with the chopped nuts (alternatively the top can be sprinkled with nuts, too).

5. Place the excess chocolate frosting into a pastry bag and pipe shells or other decorative border around the perimeter of the cake (pages 181–82). If coating the top with nuts, do not add a border, as it will not stick to the nuts. To smooth the bottom edge, hold the cake in one hand and pat the bottom with the other hand. Refrigerate until 30 minutes before serving.

Can Prepare Ahead

REFRIGERATED, 2 DAYS; FROZEN, 3 MONTHS

Makes 10 to 16 servings

Strawberry Brown Sugar Cake

USING BROWN SUGAR IN THE GENOISE AND BUTTERCREAM TRANSFORMS THIS PASSOVER STRAWBERRY SHORTCAKE INTO SOMETHING TRULY SPECIAL. COMBINED WITH THE STRAWBERRY STARBURST CROWN, THE CAKE IS A REAL SHOWSTOPPER.

PAREVE

1 recipe Passover Génoise, page 77, baked in two 8-inch round cake pans, see directions below (can be prepared 3 days in advance)

1 recipe Sabayon Brown Sugar Frosting, page 137 (can be prepared 4 days in advance)

1 recipe Strawberry Filling, page 143, see directions at right (can be prepared 2 days in advance)

104

GARNISH

1 quart fresh strawberries, washed, dried, and hulled

1. Make the génoise using brown sugar instead of the regular sugar. Cool. Set 1 layer on a 9-inch round cake board.

2. Place some of the frosting in a pastry bag with a medium star tip and pipe a line of buttercream around the perimeter of the top of the cake to hold in the filling (pages 181–82). Freeze the cake for 15 minutes to firm up the buttercream.

3. Reserve ¼ cup of clear glaze from the filling. Fill the center with half of the berry filling. Top with the second layer. Repeat the piping and filling as above.

4. With a medium star tip, pipe columns up the sides of the cake going no higher than the top edge of the cake.

5. Cut the strawberries vertically into thin slices.

6. Place the first row of berries along the perimeter of the cake with the berries pointing toward the edge of the cake. The second row should overlap the first a little, and the tips can be placed between two berries of the first row. Continue until the whole top is covered. The design should look like a starburst (page 196).

7. Add 1 teaspoon of water to the reserved glaze and reheat it over medium heat. Brush the glaze over the berries. Refrigerate. Let the cake stand at room temperature for 1 hour before serving.

Can Prepare Ahead

REFRIGERATED, 1 DAY; FROZEN 3 MONTHS

The berries will look best if served within 5 hours of cutting.

Makes 8 to 10 servings

Chocolate Mousse Cake

CAKE MUST BE ASSEMBLED 1 DAY BEFORE SERVING

PAREVE OR DAIRY

½ recipe Passover Génoise, page 77, baked in two 8- or 9-inch round cake pans, for 12 to 15 minutes (can be prepared 3 days in advance)

COFFEE SOAKING SYRUP

½ cup brewed coffee

¼ cup sugar

1 vanilla bean

FILLINGS—CHOOSE 1 (CAN BE PREPARED 3 DAYS IN ADVANCE)

Easy Dark Chocolate Mousse (dairy), page 150

Neoclassic Chocolate Mousse (pareve), page 139

1. Place both cake layers on cake boards that are the same size as the cakes. Freeze one layer and place the other on the bottom part of a 10-inch springform pan. Slide the springform sides over the cake.

2. To make the syrup, place the coffee, sugar, and vanilla bean in a small saucepan over medium heat and cook just until the sugar dissolves. Scrape out the seeds from the vanilla bean and add them back to the syrup along with the empty bean. Place in the refrigerator to cool.

3. Using a pastry brush, dab on half of the syrup.

4. If using the Neoclassic Mousse, reserve and refrigerate 1 cup of the mousse. For either mousse, proceed with the recipe.

5. Place ⅓ of the mousse on top of the cake. Remove the second layer from the freezer, remove the cake board, and place the cake on top of the mousse layer. Brush with the remaining syrup and top with ⅓ of the mousse. Smooth the top with a spatula. Use the remaining ⅓ of the mousse to fill in the space around the cake. Cover the top with plastic wrap, and refrigerate overnight.

6. In the morning, heat a knife or decorating spatula under hot water. Dry it and run it around the outside of cake. The springform can now be removed.

1 cup heavy cream

2 tablespoons vanilla sugar or
substitute, page 18

DECORATING (WITH DAIRY GARNISH)

7. Combine the cream and sugar in a mixer bowl, and refrigerate
for 15 minutes to dissolve the sugar. Put the beater blade(s) in the
refrigerator also. Beat the cream on high until stiff peaks form. Put
the whipped cream in a pastry bag with a medium open star tip and
pipe shells on the top and around the base of the cake (page 181).

DECORATING (WITH PAREVE GARNISH)

8. Let the reserved mousse come to room temperature. Lightly
beat it until it is smooth and creamy. Pipe stars or shells across the
top. Alternatively, pipe a shell border and fill the center with
chocolate shavings, rolls, or leaves (pages 187–89).

Can Prepare Ahead

REFRIGERATED, 3 DAYS; FROZEN, 3 MONTHS

*Frozen cake should be defrosted overnight in the refrigerator and then left at
room temperature 1 hour before serving.*

Makes 8 to 10 servings

107

Almond Cherry Layer Cake

CHERRIES AND ALMONDS ARE A CLASSIC COMBINATION FOR A GREAT NON-CHOCOLATE CAKE. THE SLIGHTLY PINK FROSTING AND CHERRIES ADORNING THE TOP MAKE FOR GREAT EYE APPEAL.

PAREVE

1 recipe Almond Sponge Cake, page 81 (can be prepared 2 days in advance)

1½ recipes Marinated Cherry Filling, page 141, thickened with 5 teaspoons potato starch (can be prepared 2 weeks in advance)

1 recipe Meringue Buttercream, page 131, vanilla flavored, made with 2½ sticks margarine (can be prepared 4 days in advance)

108

1. Place one of the cake layers on a cake board. Freeze the other layer to make it easier to handle.

2. Drain cherries, reserving sauce. Add ½ cup of the lightly thickened cherry sauce to the buttercream. Spread or pipe a ⅛-inch layer of buttercream onto the first layer. Press 1 cup of the cherries into the filling. Top with the second cake.

3. Use a cake-decorating spatula to spread a thin layer of the buttercream onto the sides and into the gap between the two layers of cake. Spread about ¼ inch of frosting over the top. Transfer the cake to a serving platter.

4. Put the remaining buttercream in a pastry bag with a medium star tip. Pipe contiguous vertical columns up the sides of the cake, tapering the column as it reaches the top of the cake. As the column reaches the top of the cake, round the edge so that the column actually ends on top of the cake (an alternate decoration would be to spread a thicker layer of frosting onto the sides and then coat with toasted almonds).

5. Around the top perimeter of the cake (on top of the ends of the columns) pipe a line of frosting with the star tip. Pipe three evenly

spaced lines on the top to create four chambers for the cherries.
Use a teaspoon to fill the spaces with the cherries.

Can Prepare Ahead

——

REFRIGERATED, 2 DAYS

Remove the cake from the refrigerator 1 hour before serving.

Makes 8 to 12 servings

Apricot Walnut Pavé

SOAKING SYRUP

1 cup water

½ cup sugar

2 tablespoons orange juice

CAKE

1 recipe Spongy Base Layer,
page 85 (can be prepared 3
days in advance)

1 recipe Apricot Filling, page
145 (can be prepared 1 week in
advance)

1 recipe Meringue Buttercream,
page 131, vanilla flavored (can
be prepared 3 days in advance)

½ cup chopped walnuts

GARNISH
(OPTIONAL)

2 cups chopped walnuts

1. Make the soaking syrup by combining the water and sugar in a small saucepan. Heat on medium until the sugar dissolves. Add the orange juice and set aside to cool (can be made 2 weeks ahead).

2. If the cakes have been frozen, let them stand at room temperature for 1 hour. It is okay if they are not completely defrosted. Trim the edges off all sides of each layer. Cut each cake to 9 × 14 inches. Cut each layer in half lengthwise so that there are now 4 layers, each 4 ½ × 14 inches. (If the length of this cake is a problem in terms of a serving platter, cut the layers in half widthwise to make four rectangles, each 9 × 7 inches. This is a good size especially if you are taking the cake somewhere, because it will fit in a 10-inch cake box or on almost any serving plate. Call it an apricot rectangle instead of a pavé.)

3. Cut a cake board so that it is slightly smaller than the layers, and place it under one layer.

4. Brush the first layer with ¼ of the syrup. Spread ⅓ of the apricot filling over the cake. Place another cake layer on top and brush with ¼ of the syrup. Spread a ⅛-inch-thick layer of the vanilla buttercream over the cake. Sprinkle ½ cup chopped nuts over the buttercream.

5. Add another layer of cake, brush with syrup, and spread the top with ⅓ of the apricot filling. Reserve the remaining apricot filling for decorating, or freeze for future use. Brush the last layer of cake with the syrup, and place it syrup side down on top of the filling. Use a cake-decorating spatula to remove excess filling from the sides and to fill any spaces that are lacking in filling. Freeze the cake for 15 minutes to firm it up. If the layers are not lined up nicely, trim off the ends to make the edges even.

6. If the frosting has been refrigerated, bring it to room temperature by heating it in the microwave on the lowest setting (must be lower than defrost; no. 1 is best), stirring every 10 to 15 seconds. Rebeat until smooth and fluffy. Spread the frosting on the sides and top of the cake and smooth with a cake-decorating spatula. Press the chopped nuts onto the sides of the cake.

7. If you wish to garnish with an apricot rose use the same technique as for pear flowers, page 171. If the apricots have been dried whole, cut in half where they have been pitted. Place sticky side down on waxed paper. Cover with plastic wrap and pound into oval shapes until very thin, especially along the edge that will form the petal. For the center bud, roll one apricot half sticky side in. Place the petals just like the pear petals. Roll the edges of the petals outward and fan the petals where they join each other to make them look more realistic.

Can Prepare Ahead

REFRIGERATED, 3 DAYS; FROZEN, 3 MONTHS
Defrost frozen cake in the refrigerator overnight and then leave at room temperature 1 hour before serving.

Makes 12 to 15 servings

111

Black Forest Cake

BLACK FOREST CAKE MUST BE MADE 1 DAY IN ADVANCE.
THIS CAKE WILL USE ONLY 2 LAYERS OF THE CHOCOLATE
PECAN CAKE, SO THE THIRD LAYER CAN
BE SAVED FOR ANOTHER RECIPE, OR YOU CAN
REDUCE THE RECIPE BY A THIRD.

1. Remove 1 cup of the soft buttercream and place back in the refrigerator. Put the remaining buttercream in a mixer bowl. Beat in the margarine a tablespoon at a time until the filling starts to look curdled and then forms a smooth buttercream (see instructions with Meringue Buttercream—it may need to be refrigerated). Set aside.

2. Drain the cherries and reserve the juice for another purpose.

3. Place the cakes on cake boards. Freeze one of the layers to make it easier to handle. Spoon the refrigerated, soft buttercream on the cake so that it is about ¼ inch thick. Press the cherries into the filling. Place the second cake layer on top of the cherries.

4. Thinly spread the reserved firm buttercream on the sides and top of the cake, filling in the gap between the layers.

5. Place the remaining buttercream in a pastry bag with a medium star tip and pipe contiguous stars over the entire top and sides of the cake.

PAREVE

1 recipe Meringue Buttercream, page 131, vanilla, made with 2 sticks margarine, cold (can be prepared 4 days in advance)

1 recipe Marinated Cherries, page 141 (can be prepared 2 weeks in advance)

½ stick unsalted pareve Passover margarine, at 62°F (cool and pliable)

1 recipe Chocolate Pecan Cake, page 79, baked in three 9-inch round cake pans; reduce baking time to 18 to 25 minutes (can be prepared 1 day in advance)

VARIATIONS

Dairy: Use whipped cream instead of buttercream.

Chocolate Black Forest Cake: For pareve, use Sabayon Chocolate Frosting, dark chocolate variation, page 135; for dairy, prepare Ganache Frosting, page 148, instead of the vanilla buttercream (or the center can be buttercream and the outside chocolate). Ganache can either be poured over, or you can refrigerate it until it is spreadable and use the same way as the buttercream.

Can Prepare Ahead

REFRIGERATED, 1 DAY
Store the cake in the refrigerator. Remove from the refrigerator 30 minutes before serving.

Makes 8 to 10 servings

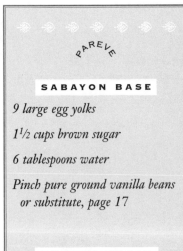

SABAYON BASE

9 large egg yolks

1 1/2 cups brown sugar

6 tablespoons water

Pinch pure ground vanilla beans
or substitute, page 17

BUTTER PECAN FILLING

1/2 cup pareve Passover semisweet
chocolate, chopped (chips are
fine)

1 cup pecan pieces, toasted and
chopped (combination of medium and fine)

3 sticks unsalted pareve Passover
margarine, room temperature

Chocolate Butter Pecan Roll

THE SABAYON WILL BE BEATEN WITH A PORTABLE
ELECTRIC BEATER WHILE COOKING ON THE STOVE;
THEREFORE, EXCESS CORD SHOULD BE HELD TAUT
TO PREVENT BURNING THE CORD. TO AVOID BEING
BURNED BY STEAM FROM THE DOUBLE BOILER, USE
A POT HOLDER MITT. (THIS RECIPE IS FEATURED ON
THE COVER.)

1. Fill the bottom of the double boiler with 2 inches of water and
bring it to a boil. Reduce the heat to medium high. Place the egg
yolks in a large metal bowl (preferably with a handle). The top of
the double boiler can be used, but it is not ideal because egg can
get stuck on the interior ledge and may overcook.

2. With a wire whisk, whisk the egg yolks just to blend, and
gradually whisk in the brown sugar, water, and vanilla powder.

3. Place the bowl over the boiling water and beat with a portable
electric mixer on medium speed for 3 minutes. Increase the speed
to high, and continue to beat for 4 minutes. The timing is important, because salmonella bacteria will be killed if cooked at 140°F
for at least 4 minutes (it takes about 3 minutes to get the eggs
up to 140°F).

4. Remove the bowl from the heat. Beat on high speed until the
eggs are cool (about 7 minutes). You can speed this up by placing
the bowl in a pan of ice water. If you prefer to transfer the eggs
to a standing mixer, use the flat beater and beat on medium high.
Remove 2/3 of the sabayon base and set aside for the butter
pecan filling.

SABAYON CHOCOLATE FROSTING

12 ounces pareve Passover semi-sweet chocolate, ground finely

$^1/_2$ cup boiling water

2$^1/_2$ sticks unsalted pareve Passover margarine, room temperature

CAKE

1 recipe Cocoa Cake Roll, page 86, baked and cooled (can be prepared 4 days in advance)

FOR THE CHOCOLATE FROSTING

5. Place the double boiler bottom back on a burner over low heat. In the top of the double boiler place the grated chocolate. Pour the boiling water over the chocolate, place on top of the hot water, and stir until the chocolate is melted and smooth. Set aside to cool.

6. Beat the margarine into the smaller portion of sabayon until smooth and fluffy. Stir in the cooled melted chocolate.

FOR BUTTER PECAN FILLING

7. To the remaining sabayon, beat in the 3 sticks of margarine, tablespoon by tablespoon, and beat until fluffy. Stir in the nuts and chopped chocolate. (Both of these frostings can be prepared ahead. For the butter pecan frosting, reserve the nuts and chocolate. Before using, bring the buttercream to room temperature, rebeat it until fluffy, and then add the reserved nuts and chocolate to the butter pecan frosting.)

ASSEMBLY

8. Spread the butter pecan filling over the cake. Roll up the cake from one short end using the extended parchment to help roll it. Roll the cake onto a cake board or pan that can be placed in the freezer. Spread the dark chocolate frosting evenly over the outside of the roll. Leave the ends for the time being.

9. Touch the tip of a cake-decorating spatula or fork to the frosting and pull up quickly to make little spikes in the frosting. The spikes can be random or done in a pattern. Continue until the whole cake is covered with spikes. Freeze the cake for $^1/_2$ hour. (To decorate like the photo on the cover, swirl the frosting into peaks using a cake-decorating spatula.)

10. When the cake is firm, the ends of the cake can be neatly sliced off, or the ends can be coated with the dark chocolate frosting and spiked. Both make nice presentations. Refrigerate until 1 hour before serving.

Can Prepare Ahead

———

REFRIGERATED, 3 DAYS; FROZEN, 3 MONTHS

———

Makes 10 to 12 servings

Chocolate Noisette Layer Cake

PAREVE

1 recipe (2 layers) Chocolate Pecan Cake, page 79, baked and cooled (can be prepared 1 day in advance)

1 recipe Noisette Fluff Frosting, page 134, reserve 1 cup of Marshmallow Meringue (can be prepared 1 day in advance)

DECORATING CHOCOLATE (OPTIONAL)

1 ounce pareve Passover chocolate, chopped

2 teaspoons vegetable oil

VARIATIONS

Make a cake roll using Cocoa Cake Roll, page 86. Use Noisette Fluff inside, and for the outside use Meringue Buttercream Frosting (light chocolate) page 131. For a fun decoration, sponge on chocolate embossing liquid, page 183, using a new Teflon ball scrubber.

1. Place one of the layers on a cake board that is smaller than the cake. Set on a cake-decorating turntable. Spoon on frosting ½ inch thick. Top with the remaining layer. Spread frosting thinly on the sides and ½ inch thick on the top.

2. Place the chocolate and oil in a small microwave safe bowl and microwave on medium for 30 seconds. If the chips look shiny, stir. If not, microwave for another 30 to 60 seconds, checking every 15 seconds until the chips are shiny. Stir and microwave in 10-second bursts until completely melted and smooth. The chocolate should be runny enough to drip off of a fork. If not, add ½ teaspoon more oil, stir, and check.

3. Place a fork into the chocolate. Hold it over the cake and rapidly shake your hand side to side to create a spatter design. Repeat until the whole cake is spattered to your liking.

4. Place the reserved meringue into a pastry bag with a medium star tip, and pipe a shell border around the top and bottom edges of the cake (decorating tips, pages 181–82). Refrigerate until 1 hour before serving.

117

Can Prepare Ahead

REFRIGERATED, 1 DAY; FROZEN, 3 MONTHS

Makes 8 to 10 servings

Hazelnut Custard Cake

DAIRY

1 cup heavy cream

2 tablespoons sugar

1 recipe Hazelnut Génoise, page 77, baked in two 10-inch round cake pans (can be prepared 2 days in advance)

1/2 cup pure maple syrup mixed with 1 tablespoon water

1 recipe Crème Patissière, page 151, cold (can be prepared 4 days in advance)

1 recipe Ganache Glaze, page 148 (can be prepared 1 week in advance)

1 1/2 cups skinned hazelnuts, page 16

1. Combine the cream and sugar in a large mixer bowl and place in the refrigerator along with the beater blade(s) for 15 minutes.

2. Toast the hazelnuts in a 350°F oven for 5 to 10 minutes or until aromatic. Place in the freezer for 5 to 10 minutes to cool. Finely chop by hand or in a food processor.

3. Place 1 cake layer on a 9-inch cake board. Using a pastry brush, dab half of the maple syrup onto the cake.

4. Whip the cream to stiff peaks and fold it into the crème patissière. Spoon the crème patissière to within 1/2 inch of the edge of the cake.

5. Brush the other layer cake with the maple syrup and place it on top of the crème patissière with the syrup side down. If the edges do not line up nicely, use a small knife to trim them. Remove any crème that may have spilled out of the cake. Cover with plastic wrap and refrigerate for several hours or overnight.

DECORATIONS

6. Make the glaze, or if it has been stored, rewarm it by placing it over hot (just under simmering) water, or by microwaving it on low until it has liquefied.

7. Place the cake on a rack over a tray with sides. Pour the glaze through a fine mesh strainer into the center of the cake. Tip the cake, if necessary, to make the glaze flow down the sides.

*2 ounces Passover chocolate,
grated (white or milk chocolate
can be used)*

*1 to 2 teaspoons mild vegetable
oil*

10 to 12 whole hazelnuts

8. When the chocolate stops dripping from the bottom of the cake,
remove the rack from the pan (you don't want to get nuts into the
extra ganache). Pat the nuts onto the sides of the cake by scooping
some nuts into your cupped palm and placing the pinkie edge of
your hand at the bottom of the cake. Then move upward as you pat
on the nuts. In this way the nuts will be preceding you and you
won't end up with chocolate all over your hands. Lift up the cake
(on its board) and pat the nuts at the bottom of the cake to make a
nice clean edge. Refrigerate the cake several hours until the glaze is
firm. Place the remaining ganache in a mixer bowl, cover, and
refrigerate several hours until firm.

9. If not making the optional embossed design and tipped
hazelnuts, skip to step 10.

For an embossed design, combine the chocolate and oil (listed
under optional decorations) in a microwavable bowl. Heat in the
microwave on medium for 30 seconds. Stir. Continue to heat and
stir in 10-second bursts until the chocolate is completely melted
and the liquid is smooth. Alternatively, heat chocolate and oil over
hot, but not simmering, water. Stir and heat until melted and
smooth. Place the glaze in a pastry bag with a very small round
(plain) tip. Pipe a design of your choice—zigzags, dots, loops, etc.
(chocolate can also be drizzled from a fork or spoon). Remove the
tip from the pastry bag and squeeze the extra chocolate into a small
bowl. Dip just the tips of the whole hazelnuts into the liquid. Set
aside on a piece of waxed paper with the glazed side up.

10. Remove the ganache from the refrigerator. If it is neither
runny nor hard, spoon it into a pastry bag with a medium star tip
and pipe a border around the top perimeter of the cake. If the
ganache is too runny, refrigerate or freeze until firmer. If too hard,

the glaze can be heated in the microwave on low power in 10-second bursts until it is soft enough to pipe. Don't forget to stir between heat bursts to distribute the heat.

11. If using the optional hazelnuts place them on the tail of every second shell. Serve the cake cold.

Can Prepare Ahead

REFRIGERATED, 2 DAYS; FROZEN, 3 MONTHS

Makes 10 to 12 servings

Tiramisu

TIRAMISU IS A TRADITIONAL ITALIAN DESSERT THAT HAS AS MANY VARIATIONS AS THERE ARE BAKERS. FOR A YEAR-ROUND VERSION, YOU CAN USED PACKAGED LADYFINGERS AND RUM, MARSALA, OR KAHLUA IN THE FILLING. MASCARPONE IS TRADITIONALLY USED IN PLACE OF THE CREAM CHEESE/BUTTER MIXTURE. ALL OF THESE VARIATIONS ARE SURE CROWD-PLEASERS. MUST BE MADE 1 TO 2 DAYS AHEAD.

DAIRY

ZABAGLIONE FILLING

¼ cup brewed coffee, cold

6 large egg yolks

1 cup sugar

1 pound cream cheese, room temperature

4 ounces (1 stick) unsalted butter, room temperature

1 cup heavy whipping cream

SOAKING SYRUP

1½ cups brewed coffee, hot

¼ cup sugar

1 tablespoon Passover brandy (optional)

CAKE

32 ladyfingers, page 83, toasted

GARNISH

6 ounces Passover chocolate, grated, page 11

1. For zabaglione, place about 1½ inches of water in the bottom of a double boiler and bring to a boil. In a metal bowl (preferably with a handle) or in the top of the double boiler, whisk the coffee and egg yolks. Gradually whisk in the sugar.

2. Set the bowl over the boiling water, over medium-high heat, and beat the eggs on medium speed for 3 minutes. Turn heat down to medium. Beat at high speed for 4 minutes.

3. Remove the bowl from the heat and continue to beat until the bowl has cooled, about 7 more minutes.

4. Beat cream cheese with butter until well mixed. Beat whipped cream to soft peak stage (see "Egg Whites," page 13). Stir 1 cup into the cream cheese and fold in the remainder.

5. Stir 1 cup of the eggs into the cream cheese. Fold in the remainder of the eggs. Refrigerate for 3 hours or up to 2 days ahead.

6. For the syrup, combine the hot coffee with the sugar, cover and set aside to cool. Add the brandy, if using. If not assembling right away, refrigerate the syrup. Bring to room temperature before using.

121

ASSEMBLY

7. One or two days before serving, dip a ladyfinger in the soaking syrup, and then place rounded side down in a decorative 9 × 13-inch pan. Repeat with half of the ladyfingers. They should be touching each other and cover the entire bottom of the pan.

8. Spoon on half of the filling. Dip and place the remaining ladyfingers. Spoon on the rest of the filling. Smooth the top with a spatula or the back of a spoon.

9. Sprinkle the chocolate in a thick layer over the filling. Cover with plastic wrap and refrigerate at least 1 or 2 days.

10. Cut tiramisu into $2\frac{1}{2}$-inch pieces. The first piece will be hard to get out. Remove the remaining pieces with a pancake turner.

OTHER PRESENTATIONS

Individual tiramisu can be made in champagne glasses. Make several layers as directed above, but add grated chocolate on top of each layer of zabaglione. Layers will show through the glass.

To make tiramisu "pickups," use Spongy Base Layer, page 85. Place 1 layer on a cardboard rectangle. Assemble the tiramisu exactly the same as in the pan. Wrap and refrigerate for 1 or 2 days. Cut into $1\frac{1}{4}$-inch squares or with a small round cookie cutter into 50 pickups. If necessary sprinkle with more grated chocolate and place each in candy or muffin wrapper. Refrigerate until serving.

Can Prepare Ahead

REFRIGERATED, 2 DAYS

Makes 12 to 15 servings

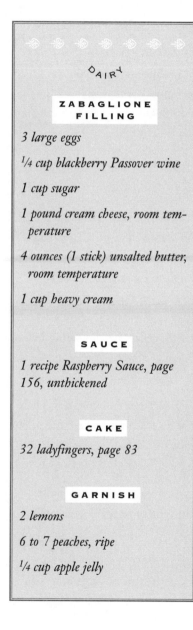

DAIRY

ZABAGLIONE FILLING

3 large eggs

1/4 cup blackberry Passover wine

1 cup sugar

1 pound cream cheese, room temperature

4 ounces (1 stick) unsalted butter, room temperature

1 cup heavy cream

SAUCE

1 recipe Raspberry Sauce, page 156, unthickened

CAKE

32 ladyfingers, page 83

GARNISH

2 lemons

6 to 7 peaches, ripe

1/4 cup apple jelly

Peach Raspberry Tiramisu

WHEN BEATING EGGS WITH A PORTABLE ELECTRIC BEATER OVER BOILING WATER, HOLD THE EXTRA CORD TAUT AND WEAR AN OVEN MITT SO THAT YOU DO NOT BURN YOURSELF.

1. Place 1 1/2 inches of water in the bottom of a double boiler and bring it to a boil. Reduce the heat to medium high. In a metal bowl (preferably with a handle) or in the top of the double boiler, whisk the eggs and the wine with a wire whisk. Gradually whisk in the sugar.

2. Set the bowl over the boiling water and beat with a portable electric beater on medium speed for 3 minutes. Keep the beater moving to prevent any egg from overcooking.

3. Turn the heat down to medium, increase the beater speed to high, and beat for 4 minutes. Remove the bowl from the heat and beat 7 minutes to cool the eggs down.

4. Beat the cream cheese with the butter until well mixed. Using a clean beater and a cold bowl, beat the whipped cream until very soft peaks form. Stir 1 cup into the cream cheese and fold in the remainder.

5. Stir 1 cup of the zabaglione into the cream cheese and fold in the remainder. Refrigerate for 3 hours or up to 2 days.

ASSEMBLY

6. Dip a ladyfinger in the raspberry sauce and place rounded side down in a decorative 9 × 13-inch pan. Repeat with half of the

123

ladyfingers. They should be touching each other and the entire bottom of the pan should be covered.

7. Spoon on half of the filling. Dip and place the remaining ladyfingers on top of the filling. Spoon on the rest of the filling. Smooth the top with a spatula or the back of a spoon. Refrigerate for 1 to 2 days.

GARNISH

8. Squeeze 1 lemon into a large bowl of cold water.

9. Boil water in a medium saucepan. Reduce heat so water is just barely simmering, and place 3 peaches into the water. Remove 1 peach and test to see if the skin will easily come off when coaxed with a knife. If not, continue heating until the peaches can be skinned. Repeat with the remaining peaches. As each peach is peeled, place it into the bowl of water that has been acidulated with the lemon. Cut peaches into wedges. Squeeze the remaining lemon over the wedges; pat them dry with paper towels. Place the peaches decoratively on top of the tiramisu.

10. Melt the apple jelly. Let cool slightly, and then brush it on the peaches. If placing the peaches more than 3 hours ahead, use apple stabilized glaze, page 192. Refrigerate until ready to serve.

11. To serve, scoop out and serve in bowls. If you wish to have a firmer tiramisu that can be cut into neat pieces, use 6 egg yolks instead of the whole eggs. Serve with extra raspberry sauce, if desired.

Can Prepare Ahead

———

Ladyfingers: REFRIGERATED, 1 WEEK;
FROZEN, 3 MONTHS

Assembled cake without peaches:
REFRIGERATED, 2 DAYS

Garnished cake: REFRIGERATED, 3 HOURS,
OR 8 HOURS IF GLAZED

———————

Makes 12 to 15 servings

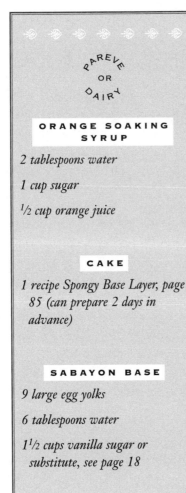

PAREVE OR DAIRY

ORANGE SOAKING SYRUP

2 tablespoons water

1 cup sugar

1/2 cup orange juice

CAKE

1 recipe Spongy Base Layer, page 85 (can prepare 2 days in advance)

SABAYON BASE

9 large egg yolks

6 tablespoons water

1 1/2 cups vanilla sugar or substitute, see page 18

Almost Seven Layer Cake

CAKE MUST BE MADE AT LEAST 1 DAY AHEAD.

1. Make the soaking syrup by combining the water and sugar in a small saucepan. Heat and stir over medium heat until the sugar dissolves. Add the orange juice, and set aside to cool.

2. Make the Sabayon base following the instructions on page 135.

FOR THE LIGHT CHOCOLATE FROSTING

3. Put an inch or two of water in the bottom of a double boiler and bring it to a simmer. Lower heat so that the water is hot, but no longer simmering. Place the chocolate in the top of a double boiler. Add the boiling water and stir until the chocolate is melted. Set the pan over the hot water and continue to stir until the chocolate is completely melted and smooth.

4. Remove 1/3 of the sabayon base and set aside. Into the larger portion of sabayon remaining in the bowl, beat in the 4 sticks of margarine until light and fluffy. Stir in the melted chocolate and set aside.

FOR THE DARK CHOCOLATE FROSTING

5. Melt the chocolate and water following the instructions above. Beat 3 sticks of margarine into the remaining sabayon base, and stir in melted chocolate.

ASSEMBLY

6. If the cake has been frozen, let it stand at room temperature for 1 hour. Trim 1/4 inch off all sides of each sponge cake. Cut each

LIGHT CHOCOLATE FROSTING

6 ounces pareve Passover semi-sweet chocolate, finely grated

¼ cup boiling water

4 sticks (1 pound) unsalted pareve Passover margarine, room temperature

DARK CHOCOLATE FROSTING

15 ounces pareve Passover semi-sweet chocolate, finely grated

½ cup plus 2 tablespoons boiling water

3 sticks (12 ounces) unsalted pareve Passover margarine, room temperature

layer crosswise into 3 strips, each $3\frac{1}{2} \times 8\frac{1}{2}$ inches (discard the 1-inch strip left at the end).

7. Cut a rectangular cake board so that it is ¼ inch larger than the cake. Set one of the layers on the board.

8. Using a pastry brush, dab on about ⅛ cup of the soaking syrup. Smooth on a thin layer of light chocolate frosting (about 1/16 inch thick). Repeat with the remaining layers. Dab the last layer with syrup before placing it on the cake, and place it with the brushed side down. Do not put frosting on the last layer.

9. Smooth the sides of the cake using extra filling to fill any gaps between the layers. Reserve any extra filling to use for decorating. Freeze the cake for 15 minutes, or refrigerate until the filling is firm. Remove from the freezer. If the layers are not lined up nicely, use a long knife to trim the cake.

10. Spread the dark chocolate frosting on the sides of the cake and then on the top. Use a good amount of frosting on the top and do not spread it very thinly, or crumbs will get caught in the frosting, making it difficult to spread. The frosting may harden as you work. This is fine and will actually help keep crumbs from getting caught.

11. To finish decorating the top, place another layer of frosting on top of the hardened layer. To make the top smooth, use a long cake-decorating spatula. Heat it under hot water, dry, and then glide it along the top to smooth the frosting.

12. An optional ridged decoration can be made by gliding a long serrated knife or cake-decorating ruler along the top to make ridges in the frosting.

127

13. Pipe stars or shells along the edge of the cake and, if desired, in lines every 1¼ inches along the top. Pipe stars along the bottom edge of the cake to conceal the cake board.

14. Refrigerate the cake for at least 1 day and preferably 2 days before serving. To serve, cut the cake into ¾-inch slices.

Can Prepare Ahead

———

REFRIGERATED, 2 DAYS; FROZEN, 3 MONTHS

Makes 8 to 10 servings

11

Frostings, Fillings, and Glazes

*O*nce you try the recipes in this section, you will never go back to the sweet and gritty frostings made with confectioner's sugar. My favorite toppings are Ganache and Caramel Topping, and for the ultimate in decadence, use them together!

MARSHMALLOW MERINGUE AND BUTTERCREAM   131

NOISETTE FLUFF FROSTING   134

SABAYON CHOCOLATE FROSTING   135

SABAYON BROWN SUGAR FROSTING   137

NEOCLASSIC CHOCOLATE MOUSSE   139

MARINATED CHERRY FILLING   141

RASPBERRY FILLING   142

STRAWBERRY FILLING   143

LEMON CURD   144

APRICOT FILLING   145

CARAMEL TOPPING   146

WHIPPED CREAM   147

GANACHE FROSTING AND GLAZE   148

EASY DARK CHOCOLATE MOUSSE   150

CRÈME PATISSIÈRE   151

PEANUT BUTTER MOUSSE FILLING   153

Meringue Buttercream Frosting

Buttercream frostings are usually made by boiling a sugar syrup to 248°F (hard ball stage) and then very carefully adding this to beaten eggs. This is a difficult process with many pitfalls. The syrup must be cooked to precisely the right temperature. If the syrup hits the beaters as it goes into the frosting, there will be hard lumps in the frosting. It is almost impossible to do this with a portable beater because you need one hand for the beater, one hand to pour in the syrup, and another hand to hold the bowl still. In addition, working with sticky sugar syrup can be very messy. The only way to get sticky syrup off of beaters, bowls, pots, and counters is to pour boiling water over the mess and let it sit until dissolved.

In my method, the eggs and sugar are beaten over boiling water to 140°F for seven minutes. There is no mess, as in the former method, any salmonella present will still be killed, and the resulting buttercream is very stable. The only minor drawback is that you must be very careful to keep the electrical cord away from the burner.

When cooking eggs over boiling water, a metal bowl with a handle works better than the top of the double boiler, because egg tends to get trapped along the ledge of the boiler top. The handle makes the hot bowl easier to hold.

Whenever possible, use unsalted butter in place of the margarine, as you will have a far superior flavor. Margarine, however, is easier to work with because it is soft even when cold, and therefore blends better with the eggs, even if it is not at the perfect temperature. The eggs must cool to room temperature, and the butter must warm to room temperature or the buttercream will be either too runny or may curdle. If using margarine, it is easy to make a soft buttercream that can be used in place of mousse or whipped cream.

Marshmallow Meringue and Buttercream

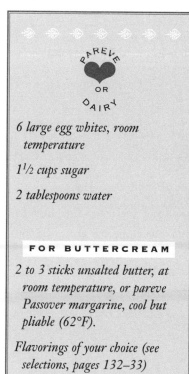

PAREVE OR DAIRY

6 large egg whites, room temperature

1¹⁄₂ cups sugar

2 tablespoons water

FOR BUTTERCREAM

2 to 3 sticks unsalted butter, at room temperature, or pareve Passover margarine, cool but pliable (62°F).

Flavorings of your choice (see selections, pages 132–33)

MARSHMALLOW MERINGUE (THROUGH STEP 4 ONLY) CAN BE USED BY ITSELF FOR A VERY LIGHT, FLUFFY FROSTING. IT SHOULD NOT BE FROZEN (UNLESS USING AS PART OF ANOTHER RECIPE), AND SHOULD BE EATEN SHORTLY AFTER ASSEMBLY.

AS YOU COOK THIS ON THE STOVE, EXCESS CORD SHOULD BE HELD TAUT. TO AVOID BEING BURNED BY STEAM FROM THE DOUBLE BOILER, USE A POT HOLDER MITT.

1. Fill the bottom of the double boiler with 2 inches of water and bring it to a boil. Reduce the heat to medium high.

2. Place the egg whites in a metal bowl (preferably with a handle). The top of the double boiler can be used, but it is not ideal because egg can get stuck on the interior ledge and may overcook. Using a wire whisk, gradually whisk the sugar and water into the egg whites.

3. Place the bowl over the boiling water and beat with a portable electric mixer on medium speed for 3 minutes. Increase the speed to high, and continue to beat for 4 minutes. The timing is important, because salmonella bacteria will be killed if cooked at 140°F for at least 4 minutes (it takes about 3 minutes to get the eggs up to 140°F). Keep the beaters moving constantly around the bowl so that egg does not overcook.

4. Remove the bowl from the heat. Beat until the eggs are cool (10 to 15 minutes). You can speed this up by placing the bowl in a

131

pan of ice water. If you prefer to transfer the eggs to a standing mixer, use the flat beater and beat on medium high. If making Marshmallow Meringue only, you are finished. Makes 6 cups.

5. To continue making buttercream, beat 2 sticks of the softened butter or margarine by tablespoonful into the cooled meringue. If using butter, go on to step 7. If using margarine, you can continue beating until the mixture is smooth and fluffy. This will yield a soft, creamy mixture that is most suitable for dolloping on the side of a rich dessert. For buttercream, continue with the next step.

6. Add another ½ stick of margarine (or 1 stick of butter) by table-spoonfuls, beating until the mixture comes together and is smooth and fluffy. If after 5 minutes the mixture still hasn't formed a buttercream, refrigerate the bowl until the mixture firms up. Beat for another 5 minutes and the buttercream should form. If the buttercream still won't form, another 1 to 2 tablespoons of margarine can be added. Chill again if necessary. If a very stiff buttercream is needed, for piping roses, for example, an additional 1 to 2 tablespoons of margarine can be added, for a total of 3 sticks of margarine or 3½ sticks of butter. This stiff buttercream should be reserved for decorations (chocolate, however, requires more butter or margarine).

7. Add the flavoring of your choice.

FLAVORINGS

Vanilla: Soften 1 vanilla bean in 2 tablespoons of hot water. Scrape out the seeds and add them to the buttercream. Let the water cool, and beat into the buttercream, as well. One of the vanilla substitutes on page 18 can also be used.

Light Chocolate: Make a half recipe of meringue and add 2½ sticks of butter or margarine to make the buttercream. Pour ¼ cup of boiling water over 6 ounces of grated chocolate and stir until melted and smooth. Stir into the buttercream. Makes about 4½ cups.

Nut: Add ¾ to 1½ cups of toasted, chopped nuts.

Raspberry: Add ½ cup Raspberry Sauce, page 156.

Coffee Buttercream: Dissolve 1 to 2 tablespoons instant coffee in 1 tablespoon boiling water. Cool, then add to buttercream.

Lemon: Add ¼ cup lemon juice and the grated zest of 1 lemon (or to taste).

Peanut Butter: Add 1 cup natural, unsalted peanut butter.

Apricot: Add ½ to 1 cup Apricot Filling, page 145, and 2 additional tablespoons frozen orange juice, defrosted.

Can Prepare Ahead

REFRIGERATED, 4 DAYS; FROZEN, 3 MONTHS

Desserts made with buttercream should be left at room temperature for about 1 hour before serving. To defrost frozen buttercream, leave at room temperature or microwave in 10-second bursts on low, stirring between heating, until soft enough to beat. Beat until soft and fluffy.

Makes about 6 cups

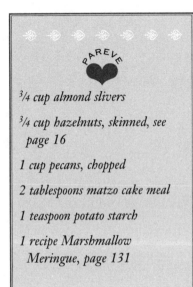

PAREVE

3/4 *cup almond slivers*

3/4 *cup hazelnuts, skinned, see page 16*

1 *cup pecans, chopped*

2 *tablespoons matzo cake meal*

1 *teaspoon potato starch*

1 *recipe Marshmallow Meringue, page 131*

134

VARIATION

Chocolate Flake: Finely chop 1 cup of semisweet chocolate and add to frosting.

Noisette Fluff Frosting

1. Place the nuts on a tray in a 350°F oven and toast until lightly browned and fragrant, about 5 minutes. Put the nuts in the freezer for 5 minutes to cool them (or leave at room temperature until cool).

2. Place half of the nuts and the matzo cake meal and potato starch in a food processor. Process until the nuts are finely chopped. Add the remaining nuts and pulse until they are coarsely chopped. Fold nut mixture into the marshmallow meringue.

Can Prepare Ahead

REFRIGERATED, 2 DAYS; FROZEN, 3 MONTHS

Makes about 6 cups

Sabayon Chocolate Frosting

SABAYON IS THE FRENCH VERSION OF A COOKED EGG "FLUFF," USUALLY MADE WITH WHITE WINE. ALTHOUGH THE WINE HAS BEEN OMITTED, THE TECHNIQUE FOR THE EGG BASE IS THE SAME AS THAT FOR SABAYON, HENCE THE NAME. TWO VERSIONS ARE OFFERED HERE. THE LIGHT VERSION HAS JUST A HINT OF CHOCOLATE AND WORKS WELL AS A FROSTING FOR A RICH CHOCOLATE CAKE OR AS THE FILLING FOR A CAKE THAT WILL HAVE A DARK CHOCOLATE FROSTING. THE DARK VERSION HAS A RICH CHOCOLATE FLAVOR AND WHEN MADE WITH MARGARINE IS A SUPERB GANACHE SUBSTITUTE.

THE SABAYON WILL BE COOKED ON THE STOVE WITH A PORTABLE ELECTRIC BEATER. CARE MUST BE TAKEN TO AVOID BURNING THE CORD. HOLD ANY EXCESS CORD TAUT AND TO AVOID BEING BURNED BY STEAM FROM THE DOUBLE BOILER, USE A POT HOLDER MITT.

135

PAREVE

DARK CHOCOLATE

15 ounces pareve Passover semi-sweet chocolate, finely grated

1/2 cup plus 2 tablespoons boiling water

3 sticks pareve Passover margarine, room temperature

LIGHT CHOCOLATE

3 ounces pareve Passover semi-sweet chocolate, finely grated

2 tablespoons boiling water

2 sticks pareve Passover margarine, room temperature

SABAYON BASE

3 large egg yolks

2 tablespoons water

1/2 cup sugar

1. Heat 2 inches of water in the bottom of a double boiler until almost simmering. Turn the heat off.

2. Choose either the dark or light variation. Place the chocolate in the top of the double boiler. Pour the boiling water over the chocolate and stir until melted. Place the pan over the hot water and continue to stir until the chocolate is completely melted and smooth. Set aside to cool.

3. Bring the water in the double-boiler bottom back to a boil; reduce the heat to medium high.

4. Place the egg yolks in a large metal bowl (preferably with a handle).

5. With a wire whisk, whisk the egg yolks just to blend, and gradually whisk in the sugar and water. Place the bowl over the boiling water and beat with a portable electric mixer on medium speed for 3 minutes. Increase the speed to high, and continue to beat for 4 minutes. The timing is important, because salmonella bacteria will be killed if cooked at 140°F for at least 4 minutes (it takes about 3 minutes to get the eggs up to 140°F). Remove the bowl from the heat.

6. Beat on high speed until the eggs are cool (about 7 minutes). You can speed this up by placing the bowl in a pan of ice water. If you prefer to transfer the eggs to a standing mixer, use the flat beater and beat on medium high.

7. Beat in the butter tablespoon by tablespoon until well blended. Stir in (do not beat) either the melted dark or light chocolate mixture until well blended.

Can Prepare Ahead

REFRIGERATED, 4 DAYS; FROZEN, 3 MONTHS

To defrost frozen buttercream, refrigerate overnight and then leave at room temperature for about 2 hours, scraping and stirring with a wooden spoon as the buttercream softens, or microwave in 10-second bursts on low, stirring between heating, until softened. Do not beat as it may cause the chocolate to get grainy.

Makes about 3 cups

Sabayon Brown Sugar Frosting

SABAYON

6 large egg yolks

¹/₄ cup water

1 cup brown sugar

FOR FROSTING

3 sticks unsalted pareve Passover margarine, room temperature

VARIATION

Butter Pecan Frosting: Add 1 cup of pecan pieces, which have been toasted at 350°F for 5 minutes or until aromatic. Chocolate flakes or chips can also be added. Makes about 3 cups.

A LITTLE CARE MUST BE TAKEN AS THE SABAYON WILL BE COOKED ON THE STOVE WITH A PORTABLE ELECTRIC BEATER. HOLD ANY EXCESS CORD TAUT TO PREVENT BURNING THE CORD. TO AVOID BEING BURNED BY STEAM FROM THE DOUBLE BOILER, USE A POT HOLDER MITT.

1. Fill the bottom of the double boiler with 2 inches of water and bring it to a boil. Reduce the heat to medium high.

2. Place the egg yolks in a large metal bowl (preferably with a handle). The top of the double boiler can be used, but it is not ideal because egg can get stuck on the interior ledge and may overcook.

3. With a wire whisk, whisk the egg yolks just to blend, and gradually whisk in the sugar and water. Place the bowl over the boiling water and beat with a portable electric mixer on medium speed for 3 minutes. Increase the speed to high, and continue to beat for 4 minutes. The timing is important, because salmonella bacteria will be killed if cooked at 140°F for at least 4 minutes (it takes about 3 minutes to get the eggs up to 140°F).

Remove the bowl from the heat.

4. Beat on high speed until the eggs are cool (about 7 minutes). You can speed this up by placing the bowl in a pan of ice water. If you prefer to transfer the eggs to a standing mixer, use the flat beater and beat on medium high.

137

5. Beat in the butter tablespoon by tablespoon until well blended. Use at once, refrigerate, or freeze.

Can Prepare Ahead

———

REFRIGERATED, 4 DAYS; FROZEN, 3 MONTHS

To defrost frozen buttercream, leave at room temperature or microwave in 10-second bursts on low, stirring between heating, until soft enough to beat. Beat until soft and fluffy.

———

Makes about 3 cups

4 large eggs

¾ cup sugar

½ cup water

8 ounces pareve Passover semi-sweet chocolate, chopped (preferably not chips)

¼ cup warm water

1½ sticks unsalted pareve Passover margarine, room temperature

Neoclassic Chocolate Mousse

"CLASSIC" CHOCOLATE MOUSSE OFTEN CONTAINS UNCOOKED EGG YOLKS, EGG WHITES, AND WHIPPED CREAM. FOR EASE OF PREPARATION, MY RECIPE USES WHOLE EGGS. THESE ARE COOKED TO MINIMIZE THE RISK OF SALMONELLA POISONING. THE CREAM IS OMITTED TO MAKE A LIGHT PAREVE DESSERT.

WHEN BEATING EGGS OVER BOILING WATER, CARE MUST BE TAKEN NOT TO BURN THE ELECTRICAL CORD OR YOURSELF. MAKE SURE THAT THE EXCESS CORD IS HELD TAUT AND USE A POT HOLDER MITT TO AVOID BEING BURNED BY STEAM.

1. Heat 2 inches of water in the bottom of a double boiler over medium-high heat.

2. In a metal mixer bowl (preferably with a handle), or in the top of the double boiler, whisk the eggs. Gradually whisk in the sugar and water.

3. With a portable electric beater, beat the eggs over the boiling water on medium speed for 3 minutes. Increase the speed to high and beat for 4 more minutes. The eggs should be very thick and pale. Make sure to keep the beater moving around the whole bowl to ensure that the eggs do not overcook. Remove from the heat. Continue to beat on high speed until the eggs cool, about 6 minutes.

4. Return the bottom of the double boiler to a low heat. The water should be hot but not simmering. Put the chocolate and water in another mixer bowl, or in the top of the double boiler (clean), and

place over the hot water. Allow the chocolate to soften and then stir with a whisk until the chocolate and liquid are smooth.

5. Remove from the heat and whisk or beat in the softened margarine, 1 tablespoon at a time. On low, beat the chocolate into the eggs.

6. Spoon into cups or a container and refrigerate. To use as a filling, beat the cold mousse until it darkens and becomes less spongy. Spread or pipe onto dessert.

Out of cup, the mousse will be best if eaten within 3 days. Stirred down and used as a filling, it can keep up to 1 week. The stirred down version can be frozen for up to 3 months. Defrost in the microwave on the lowest setting. Heat in 10-second bursts, stirring in between.

Makes 4 cups

Marinated Cherry Filling

PAREVE

2 twelve-ounce bags frozen
  cherries

1 cup sugar

$\frac{1}{4}$ cup Passover blackberry wine

$\frac{1}{4}$ teaspoon ground cinnamon

$\frac{1}{4}$ cup fresh orange juice

2 tablespoons potato starch

1. Place the cherries in a colander over a bowl and let the cherries thaw (will take several hours), or microwave on defrost for 10 to 15 minutes.

2. Place the juice that has drained from the cherries in a small saucepan, bring to a boil and cook until reduced by half. Remove from the heat and add the sugar, wine, cinnamon, and orange juice. Stir until the sugar dissolves. Pour the sauce over the cherries and refrigerate overnight or up to 2 weeks.

3. Place a colander over a bowl and pour the cherries into the colander. Place the potato starch in a small cup. Stir $\frac{1}{4}$ cup of cherry marinade gradually into the potato starch.

4. Place the remainder of the marinade in a pot and bring to a boil. Add the potato starch and cherries. Bring the mixture back to a boil, stirring constantly, and cook until thickened. Allow to cool thoroughly before covering.

Can Prepare Ahead

REFRIGERATED, 1 WEEK; FROZEN, 3 MONTHS

As with other fruit fillings, the cherries will get very soft and mushy if refrozen. Do not freeze, if possible. If you do, do not use for the top of a cake or for other decorative purposes.

Makes 1 $\frac{1}{2}$ cups

141

Raspberry Filling

PAREVE

2 twelve-ounce bags frozen
raspberries, defrosted overnight
or microwaved 10 minutes on
defrost

1 tablespoon (about 1 lemon)
fresh lemon juice

⅔ cup sugar

2 to 3 tablespoons potato starch

1. Put the berries through the fine blade of a food mill and then through a fine mesh strainer to remove all of the seeds.

2. The amount of potato starch to use will depend on how the filling is to be used and on personal taste. Three tablespoons will give a very firm filling, 2½ tablespoons a medium-firm filling, and 2 tablespoons a loose filling. Place the potato starch in a small bowl or jar. Add an equal amount of raspberry puree and stir to make a smooth paste. Add 2 more tablespoons of puree and stir until the mixture is liquid.

3. Place the remaining puree, lemon juice, and sugar in a small saucepan. Heat on medium, stirring often, until the sugar dissolves.

4. Increase heat to medium high and cook just until puree comes to a boil. Whisk in the potato starch mixture. Continue to boil until the puree "clears" (the puree will turn cloudy and whitish when the starch is added). If there are any lumps, strain through a medium mesh strainer into a container. Let cool, then cover and refrigerate until cold.

Can Prepare Ahead

REFRIGERATED, 1 WEEK; FROZEN, 3 MONTHS

Raspberry filling tends to get very "gloppy" when it is frozen. It should not be used where it needs to be decorative. To defrost, microwave on defrost, checking every 15 seconds (or leave at room temperature for several hours).

Makes 2 cups

Strawberry Filling

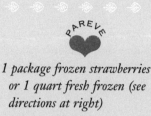

PAREVE

1 package frozen strawberries or 1 quart fresh frozen (see directions at right)

1 tablespoon lemon juice

½ cup sugar

1 tablespoon plus 1 teaspoon potato starch

1. If using fresh berries, wash and hull the berries. Cut any large berries into quarters and medium berries in halves. Freeze the berries overnight, and then proceed with the recipe. (Freezing the berries makes for a nicer consistency and makes the berries less acidic.)

2. Defrost the berries overnight or in a microwave on defrost for 10 minutes. Add the lemon juice and sugar and let sit for 15 minutes or until the sugar dissolves. Stir occasionally.

3. Place the potato starch in a small bowl. Add 3 tablespoons of the strawberry liquid, gradually, while stirring to make a smooth blend.

4. Place the strawberries and juice in a medium saucepan. Bring to a boil over medium-high heat stirring continuously. Add the potato starch mixture, bring back to a boil, and cook, stirring constantly, until the mixture thickens and clears (at first the mixture will be whitish and cloudy). Remove from the heat and cool uncovered. Use when cool or refrigerate.

Can Prepare Ahead

REFRIGERATED, 2 DAYS; FROZEN, 3 MONTHS

The strawberry filling tends to get a bit soft when refrozen. Frozen filling should not be used for the top or decorative part of a cake.

Makes 2 cups

143

Lemon Curd

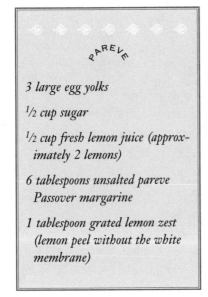

PAREVE

3 large egg yolks

1/2 cup sugar

1/2 cup fresh lemon juice (approximately 2 lemons)

6 tablespoons unsalted pareve Passover margarine

1 tablespoon grated lemon zest (lemon peel without the white membrane)

1. Before beginning to cook, have a storage container or bowl with a medium mesh strainer over it, next to the stove. Gently whisk the egg yolks just to blend. Whisk the sugar gradually into the eggs.

2. In a small noncorrosive saucepan (do not use aluminum unless you want green lemon curd), heat the lemon juice, margarine, and lemon zest over medium heat until the margarine melts. Bring liquid to a simmer.

3. Drop by drop stir the hot lemon juice into the eggs (this is called tempering, and is done so that the eggs do not scramble), stirring constantly with a wooden spoon. As the egg/lemon mixture becomes warm, the lemon juice can be added in a steady stream.

4. Return the mixture to the pot and cook over medium-low heat, stirring constantly in a figure-eight pattern. Make sure that the spoon stays in contact with the bottom of the pot and that it covers the entire bottom, so that the eggs nearest to the heat do not overcook. Cook to 160°F, just before simmering. Steam will rise from the pot and the mixture will be thick enough to coat the back of a spoon. DO NOT BOIL. If the the eggs overcook, there will be little bits of scrambled egg in the custard.

5. Strain into the storage container and refrigerate until cold.

Can Prepare Ahead

REFRIGERATED, 4 DAYS

Makes 1 cup

Apricot Filling

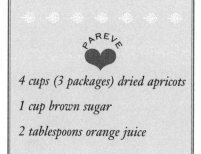

PAREVE

4 cups (3 packages) dried apricots

1 cup brown sugar

2 tablespoons orange juice

1. Cover apricots with boiling water. Cover and let sit for 1 hour to soften.

2. Reserve 2 cups of liquid from above, and drain remainder. Return the liquid to the apricots. Add the brown sugar. Bring to a simmer, cover, and cook over low heat. Stir occasionally and mash with a wooden spoon. Cook for 1 to 1½ hours until all of the apricots are soft enough to mash. If all of the liquid evaporates before the apricots are cooked, add additional water 1 tablespoon at a time and continue cooking and checking.

3. Press the apricots through the fine grater of a food mill. Stir in the orange juice. Use at room temperature or cold.

Can Prepare Ahead

REFRIGERATED, 1 WEEK; FROZEN, 3 MONTHS

Makes 2 cups

145

Caramel Topping

THIS TOPPING IS FIRM BUT NOT TOO GOOEY AND IS PERFECT FOR THE TOP OF MOLDED CAKES, SUCH AS CHEESECAKE OR BROWNIES.

DAIRY

1¼ cups sugar

5 tablespoons unsalted butter, room temperature

⅝ cup heavy cream

1. Place the sugar in a heavy, deep frying pan. Without stirring, cook over medium heat until the bottom layer of sugar has liquefied. Gently stir with a wooden spoon from the middle of the pot, drawing the unmelted sugar into the liquid caramel. Shake the pan periodically to scatter the sugar over the melted liquid. Break up any lumps with the tip of the spoon. Continue to cook and stir until all of the sugar has melted and the caramel is no longer granular, and the color is rich amber. If the caramel looks like coffee, it is burned and you will need to start over.

2. Place the butter and cream in a small saucepan. Cook over medium heat until boiling. Tip the pan of caramel away from you and add the cream mixture. The caramel will be lumpy. Return the caramel to low heat, cook and stir until the topping is melted and mostly smooth. Increase the heat to medium and boil 2 minutes. Remove any lumps.

This topping cannot be stored; it must be poured onto a dessert while still hot.

Makes a ⅛-inch topping for a 9 × 1-inch cake

Whipped Cream

1 cup heavy cream

3 tablespoons vanilla sugar or
substitute, page 18

VARIATIONS

*Chocolate: In a microwave or over
hot water, heat 2 ounces of semisweet
Passover chocolate with 1 tablespoon
of cream (from the 1 cup of cream
required). Melt according to directions on page 11. Cool to room temperature. Reduce the amount of
sugar to 2 tablespoons. Continue
with recipe. Beat the cream less
stiffly than usual and fold into the
chocolate. Use at once.*

*Roasted Nut: Roast 1/2 cup nuts in a
350°F oven for 5 to 10 minutes,
until nuts are aromatic and lightly
browned. Let cool and then process
until coarsely chopped. Add to
whipped cream.*

1. Place the cream and sugar (and vanilla if using) in a mixer
bowl and stir. Refrigerate the mixer bowl and the beater(s) for
15 minutes.

2. Remove the bowl and beater(s) from the refrigerator and beat
the whipped cream until soft peaks form when the beater is raised
out of the cream. Use a rubber scraper to turn up any cream on the
bottom that may not have been beaten well. Continue to beat the
cream carefully until stiff peaks form. You may want to do the final
beating by hand with a wire whisk because if you overbeat the
cream, you will end up with butter.

3. If you are going to spread the whipped cream on a cold cake,
underbeat it slightly, as it will continue to thicken as you spread
it around.

Can Prepare Ahead

REFRIGERATED, 3 DAYS IF DRAINED

*Whipped cream will be best if used at once, as liquid seeps out of it as it sits. If
making ahead, line a colander with coffee filters, spoon in the whipped cream, and
set this over a bowl. Refrigerate. The excess liquid will drain off and you will have
a firmer whipped cream.*

Makes about 2 cups

147

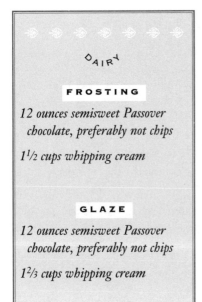

DAIRY

FROSTING

12 ounces semisweet Passover chocolate, preferably not chips

1½ cups whipping cream

GLAZE

12 ounces semisweet Passover chocolate, preferably not chips

1⅔ cups whipping cream

148

Ganache Frosting and Glaze

CONTAINING NOTHING BUT CHOCOLATE AND CREAM, GANACHE IS THE QUINTESSENTIAL CHOCOLATE FROSTING. NO OTHER FROSTING CAN MATCH ITS CHOCOLATE FLAVOR AND SMOOTH TEXTURE. USE THE BEST POSSIBLE CHOCOLATE FOR THE BEST RESULTS.

1. For frosting, put the chocolate in a food processor and process until the chocolate is finely ground.

2. Place the cream in a small saucepan and bring it to a boil over medium-high heat, stirring occasionally. Turn the processor on and pour the hot cream through the feed tube. Continue to process until the chocolate is melted and smooth.

3. Refrigerate the frosting, stirring occasionally until it is thick enough to spread. This will take several hours. The frosting can also be cooled at room temperature, then covered and refrigerated overnight. When you get ready to use it microwave it on low in 10-second bursts, stirring between until it is spreadable.

4. For glaze, grind the chocolate as above. Place cream in a medium saucepan and heat over medium-high heat, stirring occasionally until boiling. Stir in the ground chocolate and stir gently (so as not to create air bubbles) until the chocolate is melted and the glaze is smooth. Passover chocolate does not melt as quickly or as smoothly as premium chocolate.

5. Cool the glaze until a small bit of it dropped into the rest of the glaze mounds slightly and then disappears.

6. Place the dessert to be glazed on a rack over a pan. Pour the glaze through a fine mesh strainer onto the center of the cake. Keep pouring until the glaze begins to drip down the sides of the cake. Use a spatula to put glaze on any spots on the sides that are bare.

Can Prepare Ahead

REFRIGERATED, 3 MONTHS; FROZEN, 1 WEEK

Defrost frozen ganache on medium power in a microwave, stirring every 30 seconds. Alternatively, melt the ganache in a double boiler over hot water, stirring occasionally. It might be necessary to refrigerate briefly to get the right thickness.

Makes 2 cups

149

2 cups heavy cream

1/4 cup sugar

12 ounces semisweet Passover chocolate, chopped (preferably not chips)

1/2 cup whipping cream

2 tablespoons sugar

1/4 cup water

3 tablespoons mild vegetable or nut oil

VARIATIONS

If you like the bitter edge of coffee, use brewed coffee instead of water. The water can also be replaced by seedless raspberry or strawberry puree, orange juice, or fruit poaching liquid.

Dense version: **Use 1 cup of heavy cream and 2 tablespoons of sugar.**

Easy Dark Chocolate Mousse

THIS MOUSSE CAN BE MADE AS A RICH, DENSE FILLING, OR AS A LIGHTER FLUFF TO BE EATEN OUT OF A CUP. BOTH ARE EASY TO MAKE AND DELICIOUS.

1. In a mixer bowl stir together the heavy cream and sugar. Place in the refrigerator for 15 minutes.

2. Place the chocolate in a food processor. Pulse on and off until the chocolate is finely grated (this makes quite a racket—to protect ears, wear earplugs). Leave the chocolate in the processor bowl.

3. Place the whipping cream, sugar, and water in a small saucepan. Heat over medium, stirring occasionally, until the sugar dissolves. Raise heat to medium high and bring to a boil, stirring occasionally.

4. With the processor going, pour the cream through the feed tube and process until the chocolate melts. Scrape the bowl down, add the oil, and pulse a couple of times to combine. Transfer the chocolate to a medium mixing bowl. Cool to room temperature.

5. Remove the bowl of cream from the refrigerator. Beat on high until the cream mounds, just before soft peak stage. Fold the whipped cream into the chocolate until no white streaks remain. Pour into a mold or cups and refrigerate.

Can Prepare Ahead

REFRIGERATED, 4 DAYS; FROZEN, 3 MONTHS

Makes 3 to 4 cups

Crème Patissière

TRADITIONALLY, CRÈME PATISSIÈRE (PASTRY CREAM) IS MADE BY BEATING EGG YOLKS WITH SUGAR TO THE RIBBON STAGE AND THEN ADDING THE HOT MILK AND COOKING UNTIL THICK. I PREFER THIS METHOD, WHICH IS EASIER, FASTER, AND STILL RESULTS IN A RICH, SMOOTH CRÈME. IN THE CLASSICAL PREPARATION, A STICK OF BUTTER IS RUBBED ACROSS THE TOP OF THE HOT CUSTARD TO PREVENT A SKIN FROM FORMING, OR A PIECE OF PLASTIC WRAP IS PLACED ON THE SURFACE OF THE CRÈME. HOWEVER, IF BUTTER IS USED, IT HARDENS WHEN THE CRÈME IS REFRIGERATED AND MUST BE SCRAPED OFF COMPLETELY OR THERE WILL BE LITTLE BITS OF HARD BUTTER IN THE FILLING INSTEAD OF THE SMOOTHNESS THAT SHOULD EXIST. PLASTIC WRAP IS NOT WISE BECAUSE SCIENTISTS NOW BELIEVE THAT WHEN PLASTIC WRAP GETS HOT, CHEMICALS LEACH OUT OF IT AND INTO THE FOOD IT IS COVERING. THEREFORE, I LET THE SKIN FORM, AND SIMPLY SCRAPE IT OFF BEFORE USING.

DAIRY

2 cups whole milk

1 vanilla bean, split lengthwise or substitute, page 18

1/2 cup sugar, divided

6 large egg yolks

3 tablespoons potato starch

VARIATIONS

Low-Fat Crème: Use 2 percent milk and 3 whole eggs instead of the yolks.

Double Rich Crème: Whip 1/2 cup heavy whipping cream and fold into the cooled custard.

1. Place the milk, vanilla bean, and 1/4 cup sugar in a medium saucepan and heat over medium heat until boiling, stirring occasionally.

2. While the milk is heating, place the egg yolks in a medium mixer bowl and whisk lightly just to blend. Gradually stir in the sugar using a wire whisk. Sift the potato starch over the eggs and vigorously whisk to blend and remove lumps.

3. Remove the vanilla bean from the milk, cut in half, and scrape the seeds into the milk. Reserve the bean.

4. Drop by drop add the hot milk to the egg mixture, gently stirring to blend. As the mixture gets warmer, the milk can be added in a steady stream.

5. Return the mixture to the saucepan and place over medium heat. With the whisk stir in a figure-eight pattern for about 10 seconds or until the custard starts to thicken. Then stir vigorously, covering the entire bottom of the saucepan, for 1 minute. The custard should be thick and smooth.

6. Spoon the custard into a storage container (if lumps are visible before spooning, press through a medium mesh strainer into the container). Place the reserved vanilla bean back into the crème to add extra flavor. Let the crème come to room temperature, then cover and refrigerate for several hours until cold.

Before using, scrape off the top skin using a teaspoon. Remove the vanilla bean and whisk the custard to smooth and lighten the texture.

Can Prepare Ahead

REFRIGERATED, 4 DAYS

Makes 2 cups

Peanut Butter Mousse Filling

EVEN PEOPLE WHO DO NOT LIKE CREAM CHEESE
FROSTINGS WILL LOVE THIS MOUSSE. THE CHEESE AND
BUTTER PROVIDE BODY AND TEXTURE WITHOUT
DETRACTING FROM THE RICH TASTE OF PEANUT BUTTER.

DAIRY

1/2 cup heavy cream

1/3 cup vanilla sugar or substitute, page 18

1/2 cup natural creamy peanut butter, room temperature

6 ounces cream cheese (regular or 1/3 less fat), room temperature

1 stick unsalted butter, room temperature

1. Combine the cream and sugar (and extract if using). Stir and refrigerate for 15 minutes to dissolve sugar.

2. Place the cream/sugar mix and all remaining ingredients in a processor and process until smooth and fluffy.

Can Prepare Ahead

REFRIGERATED, 4 DAYS

To use cold mousse, soften in a microwave on lowest setting and then rebeat or process until fluffy.

153

Makes 1 1/2 cups

12

Sauces

Sauces are wonderful as moisteners for dry cakes such as spongecake. They can turn ordinary desserts into elegant presentations. When used with fruit, they make incredible low-fat offerings. Use these sauces year-round by substituting cornstarch for potato starch.

STRAWBERRY PUREE AND SAUCE   155

RASPBERRY SAUCE   156

MARINATED CHERRIES AND SAUCE   157

PAREVE DARK CHOCOLATE SAUCE   158

PAREVE LIGHT CHOCOLATE SAUCE   159

CRÈME ANGLAISE   160

DARK CHOCOLATE SAUCE   162

CARAMEL SAUCE   163

CARAMEL PEAR CREAM SAUCE   164

BANANA BERRY SAUCE   165

1 package frozen strawberries or
1 quart fresh strawberries

1 tablespoon lemon juice

1/2 cup sugar

Strawberry Puree and Sauce

1. If using fresh berries, wash, hull, and cut large berries. Freeze overnight (to release juices, soften the texture, and reduce the acidity).

FOR PUREE

2. Defrost the berries, and press through a food mill. Add the lemon juice and sugar. Place in a small saucepan and heat on medium just until the sugar dissolves. Chill until ready to serve.

FOR SAUCE

2. Defrost the berries in a colander over a bowl. Add the lemon juice and sugar to the strawberry juice. Place juice in a medium saucepan and heat over medium just until the sugar dissolves. Transfer to a storage container and stir in the strawberries. Refrigerate until ready to serve. For a lightly thickened sauce, follow the directions for Strawberry Filling, page 143, using only 1 to 2 teaspoons of potato starch.

Can Prepare Ahead

REFRIGERATED, 2 DAYS; FROZEN, 3 MONTHS

Makes 2 cups

155

Raspberry Sauce

PAREVE

2 twelve-ounce bags frozen
  raspberries

1 tablespoon (about 1 lemon)
  fresh lemon juice

²/₃ cup sugar

1. Place the frozen berries in a strainer over a bowl and let them defrost. Reserve the juice.

2. Put the berries through the fine blade of a food mill and then through a fine mesh strainer to remove the seeds. Add the lemon juice, and enough of the reserved raspberry juice to make a sauce the consistency you desire (thicker if it will coat a plate, and thinner if it will be used over fruit or ice cream). Add sugar to taste (²/₃ cup makes a slightly tart sauce).

3. Place the sauce in a small saucepan, and cook over medium heat until the sugar dissolves, stirring occasionally. Remove from the heat.

4. Transfer sauce to a storage container and refrigerate until cold. A lightly thickened sauce can be made by adding a little potato starch to the puree. See the directions for Raspberry Filling, page 142, but use only 1 to 2 teaspoons of starch.

Can Prepare Ahead

REFRIGERATED, 1 WEEK; FROZEN, 3 MONTHS

To defrost, microwave on defrost, checking every 15 seconds (or leave at room temperature for several hours).

Makes 2 cups

2 twelve-ounce bags frozen
cherries

1 cup sugar

$^1/_4$ cup Passover blackberry wine

$^1/_4$ teaspoon ground cinnamon

$^1/_4$ cup fresh orange juice

Marinated Cherries and Sauce

CHERRY SAUCE IS BEST SERVED OVER ICE CREAM OR
YOGURT. LIGHTLY THICKENED SAUCE CAN BE SPOONED
INTO GOBLETS WITH CRÈME PATISSIÈRE OR CHOCOLATE
MOUSSE, IN TRIFLES, AND WITH CHOCOLATE CAKE
(FOLLOW DIRECTIONS FOR MARINATED CHERRY FILLING,
PAGE 141, BUT USE ONLY 1 TO 2 TEASPOONS OF POTATO
STARCH). THE DRAINED CHERRIES CAN BE USED
BETWEEN CAKE LAYERS.

1. Place the cherries in a colander over a bowl and let the
cherries thaw several hours or overnight. Reserve the juice.

2. Place the cherry juice in a small saucepan, bring to a boil, and
cook until reduced by half. Remove from the heat and add the
sugar, wine, orange juice, and cinnamon. Stir until the sugar
dissolves.

3. Pour the sauce over the cherries and refrigerate overnight or
up to 2 weeks.

Can Prepare Ahead

REFRIGERATED, 2 WEEKS

*As with other fruit sauces, the cherries will get very soft and mushy if refrozen.
Do not freeze, if possible. If you do, do not use for the top of a cake or for other
decorative purposes.*

Makes 1$^1/_2$ cups

8 ounces pareve Passover semi-
sweet chocolate, chopped, or
chocolate chips

2 tablespoons oil

2 tablespoons honey

1 cup water

Pareve Dark Chocolate Sauce

THIS SAUCE IS DESIGNED TO BE USED FOR COATING THE
PLATE UNDERNEATH A DESSERT (AS OPPOSED TO HOT
FUDGE, WHICH GOES ON TOP OF A DESSERT).

1. Place the chocolate, oil, and honey in a microwavable bowl.

2. Bring the water to a boil. Add ¼ cup of boiling water to the
chocolate, cover, and microwave on medium heat for 15 to 30
seconds (depending on the strength and wattage of your microwave). Stir the chocolate mixture until melted and smooth.

3. The sauce needs to be thin enough to easily coat a plate. The
amount of water to use will depend on the type of chocolate used,
how it has been measured, and whether it will be used immediately
or made ahead. Most chocolates will need at least 2 to 4 more
tablespoons of water. If made ahead, add enough water to get the
sauce to coat a plate. Set aside at room temperature. Before saucing
plates, add more room-temperature water by the tablespoonful
until the sauce thins to the proper consistency. If there are any
lumps, strain through a fine mesh strainer.

Can Prepare Ahead

REFRIGERATED, 2 WEEKS

If refrigerating, microwave until room temperature.

Makes 1 cup

Pareve Light Chocolate Sauce

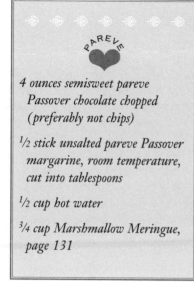

4 ounces semisweet pareve
Passover chocolate chopped
(preferably not chips)

½ stick unsalted pareve Passover
margarine, room temperature,
cut into tablespoons

½ cup hot water

¾ cup Marshmallow Meringue,
page 131

1. Bring about 1 inch of water in the bottom of a double boiler to a simmer. Reduce heat to low so that water is hot, but not simmering.

2. Put the chocolate and margarine in the top of the double boiler, place over the warm water, and heat until the chocolate melts. Stir together. Stir in the water until smooth. Remove from heat and cool to room temperature.

3. Add the meringue and stir with the wire whisk until the lumps of meringue break up and the sauce is smooth.

Can Prepare Ahead

REFRIGERATED, 2 DAYS; FROZEN, 2 MONTHS

Makes 2 cups

159

Crème Anglaise

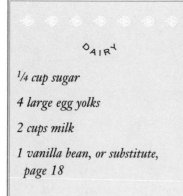

DAIRY

¼ cup sugar

4 large egg yolks

2 cups milk

1 vanilla bean, or substitute, page 18

THIS CRÈME ANGLAISE IS THINNER AND LESS RICH THAN MOST. IT WILL STILL COAT A PLATE NICELY AND WORKS WELL UNDER RICH CAKES OR TORTES. FOR A RICHER VERSION, USE UP TO TWICE AS MANY EGG YOLKS, OR SUBSTITUTE HALF-AND-HALF FOR THE MILK. THE SUGAR CAN ALSO BE DOUBLED FOR A SWEETER SAUCE.

1. Before beginning, have a 3-cup storage container (or a bowl) near the stove, with a large, fine mesh strainer over it.

2. With a wooden spoon, stir the sugar gradually into the yolks.

In a medium saucepan, over medium-high heat, heat the milk and vanilla bean to boiling. Remove from heat. Reduce the burner to medium.

3. Drop by drop, add the hot milk into the eggs (this is called tempering, and is done so that the eggs do not cook), stirring constantly with a wooden spoon. As the egg/milk mixture becomes warm, the milk can be added in a steady stream.

4. Return the mixture to the pot (including the vanilla bean) and heat over medium heat until just below boiling, stirring constantly in a figure-eight pattern. Make sure that the spoon stays in contact with the bottom of the pot and that it covers the entire bottom, so that the eggs nearest to the heat do not overcook.

5. Cook the custard until just before simmering. Steam will rise from the pot and the mixture will thicken slightly, enough to coat the back of a metal spoon. If possible use an instant-read thermometer and cook to about 160°F. DO NOT BOIL. If the

mixture boils, the eggs will overcook, and there will be little bits of scrambled egg in the custard.

6. Strain the sauce into a storage container. Scrape the vanilla seeds into the sauce and return the bean to the sauce. Cover and refrigerate until cold. Before serving, strain again to remove the skin that has formed on the top of the sauce.

Can Prepare Ahead

REFRIGERATED, 4 DAYS; FROZEN, 3 MONTHS

Makes 2 cups

Dark Chocolate Sauce

THIS SAUCE IS ALSO DESIGNED TO BE USED TO COAT A
PLATE. FOR HOT FUDGE, USE WHIPPING CREAM INSTEAD
OF THE HALF-AND-HALF AND LEAVE VERY THICK.

DAIRY

8 ounces Passover semisweet
chocolate, chopped, or chips

2 tablespoons honey

1 cup half-and-half

1. In a medium microwavable bowl, combine the chocolate and honey. Heat ½ cup half-and-half on medium heat, stirring occasionally, until boiling. Pour the hot liquid over the chocolate, cover, and microwave on medium, 15 to 30 seconds, until the chocolate is melted. Stir until smooth.

2. If using immediately, continue to add half-and-half until the sauce is thin enough to easily coat the bottom of a plate. If storing, refrigerate until ready to use. Microwave on medium in 10-second bursts until the sauce is liquidy. Add more half-and-half as necessary to make the sauce the right consistency. Strain the sauce through a fine mesh strainer.

Can Prepare Ahead

REFRIGERATED, 1 WEEK; FROZEN, 3 MONTHS

Makes 1 cup

Caramel Sauce

THE LESS CREAM USED, THE SWEETER AND THICKER THE SAUCE WILL BE. START WITH ¾ CUP. MORE CAN ALWAYS BE ADDED LATER, IF YOU DECIDE THAT A THINNER, LESS SWEET SAUCE IS DESIRED.

DAIRY

1 cup sugar

⅓ cup water

¾ to 1½ cups heavy cream

1. Combine sugar and water in medium pot. Cook over medium heat until the sugar dissolves.

2. Increase heat to medium high and boil, without stirring, until rich amber in color, 5 to 10 minutes.

3. Remove the pan from the burner. Tip the pan away from you to avoid getting burned, and add the cream. The caramel will form a lump in the bottom of the cream.

4. Return the pot to the heat and cook over medium heat until the caramel lump melts and the sauce is smooth. Remove from heat, cool, cover, and store in the refrigerator until ready to serve. Before using the sauce, stir, and strain if necessary. Sauce can also be used warm.

Can Prepare Ahead

REFRIGERATED, 1 WEEK; FROZEN, 3 MONTHS

Makes 1 to 2 cups

163

Caramel Pear Cream Sauce

THIS SAUCE IS WONDERFUL SPOONED ON POACHED PEARS, OVER ICE CREAM, AND WITH BROWNIES. IT IS USED IN THE FOLLOWING RECIPES: CHOCOLATE MOUSSE STUFFED WHOLE PEARS OR QUARTERS, PAGE 176, AND PEAR FLOWER ALMOND TORTES, PAGE 94.

DAIRY

3 cups syrup from Caramel Poached Pears, page 167

1½ to 2 cups heavy cream

1. Place the syrup in a medium saucepan and boil on high until reduced to 1 cup.

2. Add 1½ to 2 cups of cream (or to taste) to make a caramel that has the flavor you want. Bring it to a boil over medium-high heat. Transfer to a storage container and refrigerate until serving time. The sauce will separate as it sits. Be sure to stir well before serving and if there are any lumps, strain the sauce.

Can Prepare Ahead

REFRIGERATED, 1 WEEK; FROZEN, 3 MONTHS

Makes 1¾ to 2¼ cups

½ cup (1 stick) unsalted butter, cut into tablespoon size pieces

½ cup brown sugar

1 teaspoon ground cinnamon

½ cup Passover blackberry wine

3 to 4 medium bananas, just ripe

1 medium lemon

VARIATION

Substitute 3 oranges for the bananas. Peel the oranges, cut into rounds (across the equator of the orange), cut rounds into quarters, and mix into sauce.

Banana Berry Sauce

THIS SAUCE HAS A RICH BROWNED BUTTER AND CARAMEL FLAVOR WITH A BACKGROUND OF BLACKBERRY. ITS TASTE IS COMPLEX AND VERY RICH.

BANANA BERRY SAUCE GOES NICELY WITH ANY PLAIN CAKE SUCH AS ALMOND SPONGE CAKE, PAGE 81, OR A THICK LAYER OF GENOISE, PAGE 77. FOR AN ATTRACTIVE PRESENTATION, PIPE WHIPPED CREAM ON TOP OF THE CAKE AND SERVE THE SAUCE EITHER UNDER EACH SLICE OF CAKE, OR IN A PITCHER AT THE SIDE OF THE WHOLE CAKE (FOR A BUFFET).

1. Melt the butter in a large skillet over medium heat. Add the brown sugar and cinnamon and cook and stir until the sugar is melted. Add the wine and cook for about 5 minutes until the sauce has thickened. Stir, with a small whisk, in a figure-eight pattern to blend all the ingredients together into a smooth sauce.

2. Slice the bananas and squeeze the lemon over them to keep them from turning brown. Place in a small bowl, and pour the sauce over the bananas. Serve at once.

This should be made just before eating, and cannot be stored.

Makes 6 to 8 servings

165

13

Fruit

Fruits make wonderful, light, low-fat desserts suitable for any occasion. They can be served as simple family desserts or can be dressed up to fit the most formal occasions. Besides the recipes in this chapter, fruits of your choice can be doused with any of the sauces from the preceding chapter or spooned onto any of the foundation cakes (chapter 8). To round out a fruit dessert, serve with a platter of cookies or miniature pastries.

CARAMEL POACHED PEARS   167

VANILLA OR WINE POACHED PEARS   169

PEAR FLOWERS   171

NOISETTE STUFFED PEAR DAISIES   174

CHOCOLATE MOUSSE STUFFED WHOLE PEARS
OR QUARTERS   176

Caramel Poached Pears

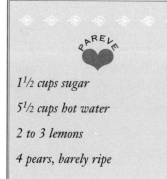

PAREVE

1½ cups sugar

5½ cups hot water

2 to 3 lemons

4 pears, barely ripe

1. Place the sugar in a large (6-quart) stainless steel or enamel saucepan (other pans may cause the pears to darken). Without stirring, cook over medium heat until the bottom layer of sugar has liquefied. Reduce heat to low and stir from the middle of the pot, drawing the unmelted sugar into the liquid caramel. Break up any lumps with the tip of the wooden spoon. Continue to gently stir until all of the sugar has melted.

2. Increase the heat to medium and stir until the caramel has liquefied and is no longer granular, and the color is rich amber. If the caramel looks like coffee, it is burned and you will need to start over.

3. Tip the pan away from you, and add the water. Be careful of the hot caramel as it steams and bubbles up. The caramel will harden when the water is added. When the steaming stops, stir and heat until all of the caramel melts again. Remove from the heat and squeeze in 2 of the lemons.

4. If making many pears, squeeze the extra lemon into a bowl of water and put the peeled, whole pears into the bowl. When all of the pears are peeled, use a slotted spoon to slide the pears into the caramel. Place over high heat until the liquid starts to boil and then reduce the heat to low so that the caramel is just barely shaking. Cover and cook the pears 5 to 45 minutes, until a sharp knife tip can be easily inserted into the pears. The amount of time will vary with the type of pear and the ripeness.

167

If pears are to be cut, rub lemon on exposed surfaces.

Cut the pears in half, core, slice, and serve in bowls with a little of the poaching syrup.

For a more elegant presentation, cut the pears in half lengthwise and remove the core. Place the pears cut side down on a cutting board. Starting ⅓ inch from the stem end, make 8 or 9 lengthwise cuts through the pears. The slices will still be attached at the stem end.

Spoon 2 to 3 tablespoons of sauce (your choice, see index) onto each dessert plate. Decorate if desired using one of the methods on pages 171–73. With a spatula, transfer pears to the plates. Use a knife to separate and fan the slices.

168

5. When the pears are done, transfer to a storage container and immediately pour the syrup over the fruit. If any of the pears are floating, ball up some aluminum foil and press into the syrup so that the pears are completely submerged in the liquid. Cool, cover, and refrigerate for up to 5 days (best in 2 days). If making Caramel Pear Cream Sauce, page 164, leave 3 cups of syrup in the pot for the sauce.

Can Prepare Ahead

REFRIGERATED, 2 DAYS

Serves 8

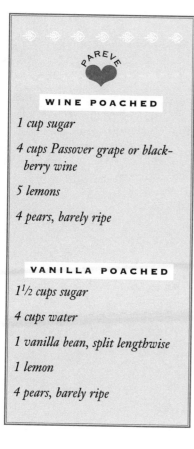

WINE POACHED

1 cup sugar

4 cups Passover grape or black-berry wine

5 lemons

4 pears, barely ripe

VANILLA POACHED

1½ cups sugar

4 cups water

1 vanilla bean, split lengthwise

1 lemon

4 pears, barely ripe

Vanilla or Wine Poached Pears

THESE PEARS CANS BE USED AS AN EASIER ALTERNATIVE TO THE CARAMEL POACHED PEARS. THE VANILLA PEARS HAVE A MORE SUBTLE, LESS SWEET FLAVOR, WHILE THE WINE POACHED PEARS HAVE A BITE TO THEM. THESE PEARS TASTE GREAT ON SIMPLE CAKES, BY THEMSELVES OR WITH SAUCES.

FOR WINE POACHED PEARS

1. Combine the sugar, wine, and ¼ cup fresh lemon juice (about 4 lemons) in a 6-quart stainless steel or other noncorrosive pot. Heat over medium heat until the sugar dissolves.

2. Meanwhile, squeeze the last lemon into a large bowl of water and drop the lemon rind into the water. Peel the pears one at a time and place them into the bowl. When all of the pears are peeled, use a slotted spoon to slide the pears into the hot liquid. Place over high heat until the liquid starts to boil.

3. Reduce the heat to low so that the wine is just barely simmering. Cover and cook the pears 5 to 45 minutes, until a sharp knife tip can be easily inserted into the pears. The amount of time will vary with the type of pear and the ripeness.

4. When the pears are done, transfer to a storage container and immediately pour the syrup over the fruit. If any of the pears are floating, ball up some aluminum foil and press into the syrup so that the pears are completely submerged in the liquid. Cool, cover and refrigerate for up to 5 days (best in 2 days).

169

FOR VANILLA POACHED PEARS

1. Follow the same instructions as for the wine poached pears, adding the vanilla bean to the liquid and the single lemon to the bowl of peeled pears.

2. Before storing the pears, scrape out the seeds from the inside of the bean and add them along with the bean to the syrup. Because there is much less lemon in this recipe, the pears are best used immediately.

Can Prepare Ahead

REFRIGERATED, 2 DAYS

Makes 4 pears

Pear Flowers

PEAR FLOWERS ARE EASIEST TO MAKE IF YOU USE FAT PEARS, SUCH AS BARTLETTS. YOU CAN MAKE SMALL FLOWERS, TO GO ON MINI-TARTS, BY USING JUST THE OUTSIDE SLICES, OR LARGER FLOWERS BY USING THE LONGER SLICES OF PEAR AND ADDING MORE ROWS OF PETALS. YOU CAN MAKE PINK ROSES BY POACHING THE PEARS IN WINE, OR TIPPED ONES BY PAINTING THE OUTSIDE OF THE PEAR (BEFORE CUTTING) WITH RED FOOD COLORING. USE 1 PEAR PER FLOWER AND SAVE THE SCRAPS FOR ANOTHER PURPOSE.

PAREVE

1 recipe Poached Pears, page 169

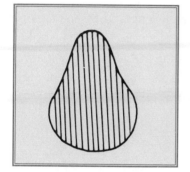

13.1

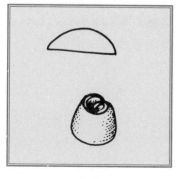

13.2

1. Cut the pears in half lengthwise and remove as little of the core as possible.

2. Pat the pears dry with paper towels. If you will not be placing the pears immediately, assemble the pears on the storage pan so that you will not have to move them more than once after they are made.

3. Bud: Cut 1 pear at a time into paper-thin lengthwise slices (*see illustration 13.1*). Start the flower with the center bud by rolling one of the small outside slices (*see illustration 13.2*). Turn it upside down so that the base is fatter than the top.

171

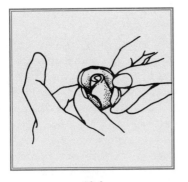

13.3

4. First row: Wrap 2 or 3 slices around the bud, overlapping slices slightly (*see illustration 13.3*).

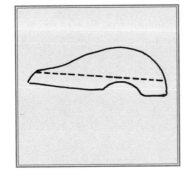

13.4

5. Second row: You will need slightly longer slices. You may need to cut the slices so they are not as high, otherwise the bud and first row will recede too far into the center (*see illustration 13.4*).

The petals of this row should be centered on the overlap of 2 petals of the previous row.

13.5

6. Third row: Continue as above, staggering the rows of petals and using longer slices as needed until you have the size flower you want (*see illustration 13.5*).

7. As you get to the outside rows of petals you can increase the number of petals per row to 5.

8. Transfer the flowers to your dessert using a spatula about the same size as the flower. You may need to do a little patching on any flowers that come apart.

STORAGE

If storing the pears more than 8 hours, use a feather pastry brush to paint them with Stabilized Fruit Glaze, page 192. Use apple jelly and thin with poaching liquid.

Serve Pear Flowers on a pool of chocolate, raspberry, or caramel sauce with a side platter of cookies or use for one of the recipes listed in the index.

Can Prepare Ahead

REFRIGERATED, 1 DAY

Makes 8 Pear Flowers

173

Noisette Stuffed Pear Daisies

PAREVE

NOISETTE FLUFF FROSTING

1 recipe Marshmallow
Meringue, page 131

1¼ cups unsalted mixed nuts

1 tablespoon matzo cake meal

½ teaspoon potato starch

PEARS

1 recipe (8 pears) Caramel
Poached Pears, page 167 (can
be made 2 days in advance)

¼ cup apple jelly

SAUCE

1 recipe Pareve Light Chocolate
Sauce, page 159

DECORATING LIQUID

1 ounce pareve Passover semi-
sweet chocolate, chopped

1 teaspoon mild vegetable oil

1. Place half of the nuts in a processor with the matzo cake meal and pulse to coarsely chop. Add the remaining nuts and pulse again.

2. Add the nuts to 2 cups of meringue. Reserve some of the remaining meringue to make the sauce. (Can be made 2 days in advance.)

ASSEMBLY OF DAISIES

3. Cut the pears crosswise into slices ½ inch thick. Cut out the center core using a 1- or 1¼-inch round cookie cutter (the size will vary depending on the diameter of the pear).

4. Use a daisy cookie cutter the same diameter as the pear slice to cut the rounds into daisy shapes. If unavailable, leave the slices round. Daisies can be cut, but not filled, 1 day in advance.

5. Brush cut daisies with melted apple jelly. If not using right away, cover with plastic wrap and refrigerate.

ASSEMBLY

6. Place 3 daisies on each plate (use dinner size), arranged to look like the eyes and nose of a face. Fill the center of each daisy with the filling. Draw a cake-decorating spatula or the back of a knife straight across the top of each daisy to level the filling.

Use Pareve Dark Chocolate Sauce, page 158, instead of the light sauce. Thin some of meringue to use for decorating.

7. Spoon the sauce around the daisies and tip the plate to cover the bottom with sauce (you cannot sauce the plates first, because the sauce leaks up around the filling and does not look appetizing).

8. In a microwavable bowl combine the chocolate and oil. Microwave on medium for 30 to 60 seconds, until the chips look shiny. When shiny, stir. If necessary, microwave in 10-second bursts until the chips are melted and the liquid is smooth.

Vine Decoration: Using a $\frac{1}{8}$ teaspoon measuring spoon, place 2 small drops of decorating liquid on each side of the single daisy. Draw a fine knife tip, skewer, or toothpick through the center of one of the drops and down through the other droplet. Repeat on the other side. The hearts should connect to form a vine. Serve immediately.

Can Prepare Ahead

REFRIGERATED, 1 DAY

Makes 8 servings

2 recipes Caramel or Vanilla
Poached Pears, pages 167, 169

**PAREVE FILLINGS
AND SAUCES**

½ recipe Neoclassic Chocolate
Mousse, page 139, softened

1 recipe Raspberry Sauce,
page 156

**DAIRY FILLINGS
AND SAUCES**

1 recipe Easy Dark Chocolate
Mousse, page 150, softened

1 recipe Caramel Pear Cream
Sauce, page 164

DECORATING LIQUID

1 recipe Blending Chocolate,
page 187

Chocolate Mousse Stuffed Whole Pears or Quarters

ASSEMBLY OF WHOLE PEARS

1. Pat the pears dry with paper towels. Hold the pear upside down so the bottom of the fat end is visible. Use a melon baller or a knife to remove the core of the pear and to create a cavity about 1½ inches in diameter and about 3 inches deep. Leave the stem attached. Put the filling in a pastry bag with a ½-inch plain tip, and fill the cavity completely.

2. The pears can be stuffed up to 1 day ahead. If preparing ahead, or if you want them to be shiny, glaze them with Stabilized Fruit Glaze, page 192. Place on a tray and cover with plastic wrap. Just before serving, spoon 2 to 4 tablespoons of sauce onto each dessert plate (depending on the size of the plate) and tip the plate so that the whole bottom is covered with sauce. Marbleize sauce using directions that follow, or use one of the techniques on page 184. Place a pear in the middle of the sauce.

ASSEMBLY OF QUARTERS

1. Dry the pears with paper towels and cut in half. Use a melon baller to cut out the seeds and make a hollow that follows the contours of the pear and goes up almost to the stem. If the pears are not soft enough, you will have to use a small sharp knife to do this. Halve each piece to form 4 hollowed-out quarters.

2. Using a medium star tip, pipe stars of mousse in a vertical line to fill the hollow of each quarter (see piping tips, page 180). Cover with plastic wrap and refrigerate until 15 minutes before serving. If making ahead, brush the exposed pear with Stabilized Fruit Glaze, page 192.

DECORATING

3. Spoon 3 to 4 tablespoons sauce onto each plate (use dinner size).

Marbleizing: Spoon or pipe decorating liquid in circles, squiggles, or cursive *e*'s. Draw a skewer, toothpick, or fine knife through the design to marbleize the liquids.

If using whole pears, place one, centered, on the plate.

For quarters, place one quarter, fat side out, at 12:00, and two others at 10:00 and 2:00, with the tips turned inward to form a fleur-de-lis.

177

Can Prepare Ahead

REFRIGERATED, 1 DAY

Makes 8 to 10 servings

14

Decorating Basics

This chapter will be useful for both the beginner and experienced baker. For the novice, it will serve as a basic primer for decorating equipment, techniques, and ideas. The more advanced baker may want to skim the chapter for information specific to Passover baking, the behavior of Passover ingredients, and equipment most suitable for Passover. For all cooks it can be used as a general decorating reference for year-round baking.

PASTRY BAGS, COUPLERS, AND TIPS   179

SAUCE AND GLAZE DECORATIONS   183

CHOCOLATE GRATINGS, CURLS, CIGARETTES, ETC.   187

CUTTING CAKES   189

DECORATING WITH FRUITS   191

FRUIT GLAZE   191

STABILIZED FRUIT GLAZE   192

14.1

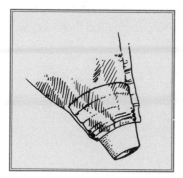

14.2

14.3

Pastry Bags, Couplers, and Tips

I like plastic disposable pastry bags because they get thrown away instead of cleaned. The ones found at craft stores are small and not very flexible, but will do for quick, small jobs. Larger, more flexible disposables can be found at suppliers listed in the appendix.

Cloth bags are more economical and better for the environment. You will need to buy them especially for Passover. You might want at least three bags: one for dairy, one for pareve, and one for piping meringue and other grease-sensitive substances. To clean cloth bags, soak them in a solution of hot water and vinegar (Passover vinegar). Dry them over a wine bottle. Cloth bags can be bought at the same places as disposable bags, but better ones are available from suppliers listed in the appendix.

Couplers

Couplers are used so that decorating tips can be attached to the outside of the pastry bag and changed without emptying the bag. To use a coupler unscrew the two parts of the coupler and place the main-part into the bag with the threaded part down. Cut off the tip of the bag until you can push the coupler through so that some, but not all, of the threads are showing *(see illustration 14.2)*. Put the tip onto the unthreaded section, and screw on the nut to hold the tip securely in place *(see illustration 14.3)*.

PIPING TECHNIQUE

To fill a pastry bag, put on the coupler and tip. Place the bag in a tall glass or pitcher (depending on the size of the bag). Fold down the top two inches of the bag. Spoon in the filling, holding the bag under the two-inch collar, if necessary. Squeeze the filling down so there is as little air in the bag as possible, by holding the bag shut with one hand and pushing down with the other hand. To use, unfold the top of the bag, twist the bag closed, and hold the twist in the crook of the thumb and index finger, pressing the fingers together to hold the bag shut. Squeeze the bag with the remaining fingers and the palm until the filling comes out of the tip. As the filling gets used it will be necessary to twist the top more to take up the extra space and to push the filling down the tube. Use the other hand to steady and guide the bag.

Tips or Tubes

Plain or round tips are used to pipe dots, mounds, beads, line decorations, and for writing. They are numbered and sized as follows:

Small tips	no. 1–4
Medium tips	no. 5–8
Large tips	no. 9–12
Extra large	no. 1A–8A

To pipe dots and mounds, hold the bag at a 90-degree angle (straight up and down). Place the tip slightly above the surface and squeeze until the dot is the size you want. Stop squeezing and pull the tip up and away. For a mound, move the tip upward as you press until the mound is the height desired. Stop pressing and pull tip up and away. Use a finger dipped in potato starch to press down the point.

For lines and line decorations, the bag is usually held at a 45-degree angle and the above technique also applies.

Star tips are used for stars, shells, rosettes, fleur-de-lis, ropes, zigzags, scrolls, etc. The most common tubes are open star tips numbered as follows:

Small	no. 13–16
Medium	no. 17–19
Large	no. 20–22
Extra large	no. 1B–8B

Follow the instructions that follow for the different shapes.

STARS: (1) Hold the bag at a 90-degree angle with the tip slightly above the surface.

(2) Squeeze filling until star is desired size and pull tip up (*see illustration 14.4*).

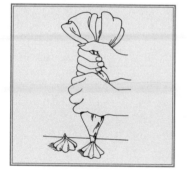

14.4

SHELLS: (1) Hold bag at a 45- to 90-degree angle with the tip slightly above the surface.

(2) Squeeze the bag and lift tip up a little as the shell forms (*see illustration 14.5*).

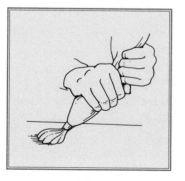

14.5

181

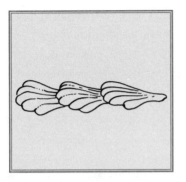

14.6

(3) Relax pressure on the bag slightly and pull the bag down closer to the surface to form the tail of the shell.

(4) Stop squeezing, and pull the tip away. Start each new shell at the tail of the previous shell *(see illustration 14.6)*.

14.7

ROSETTES: Hold bag at a 90-degree angle and squeeze out the icing, making a tight circle ending at the point where you began *(see illustration 14.7)*.

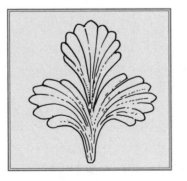

14.8

FLEUR-DE-LIS: (1) Hold bag at a 90-degree angle with the tip slightly above the surface.

(2) Pipe a shell in the center of the space you are decorating.

(3) To the left of the shell, about halfway down from the top of the center shell, and almost parallel to it, start another shell. As you pipe closer to the center shell turn your hand and pipe the tail parallel to the center, joining the tail to the tail of the center shell.

(4) Repeat on the right side to finish the fleur *(see illustration 14.8)*.

For other techniques, consult any of the Wilton cake-decorating books available from cake decorating stores, craft stores, or suppliers listed in the appendix.

Sauce and Glaze Decorations
Embossed Designs

For decorations that sit on top of glazes, allow the glaze to dry and then apply the decorations. These can be stripes, zigzags, dots, or random designs. The effect will be an embossed one with the decoration raised above the glaze. For embossed decorations, use plain melted chocolate, or if the dessert will be frozen or refrigerated, add a small quantity of oil (see below) so that the decoration will not become brittle when cold. You can use the same color or a contrasting color or mix the two for differing effects. The amount of oil to be used will depend on the type and brand of chocolate and the way in which the chocolate will be used. For example, if the chocolate is to be piped, it must be thicker than if it is to be spooned, otherwise it will run right out of the pastry bag. Chocolate chips generally require more thinning than bar chocolate.

183

2 ounces semisweet Passover bar chocolate, grated

1 to 2 teaspoons oil

EMBOSSING CHOCOLATE

In a microwavable bowl combine the chocolate and oil. Heat in the microwave on medium for 30 seconds. As the chocolate starts to melt it will look shiny. If not yet melting, continue to heat in 10-second bursts until it begins to shine. Stir. Continue to heat and stir until all of the chocolate has melted into a smooth liquid. It is essential to heat gently and stir so that the chocolate will melt evenly and will not scorch in some spots while other pieces remain unmelted. Alternatively, heat chocolate and oil over hot, but not simmering water. Stir and heat until melted and smooth.

Blended Designs

Glazes must be freshly poured and wet for a blended decoration. Blending can be done on a wet chocolate glaze or on a dessert sauce. When decorating with chocolate on a sauce, the sauce must be warm or at room temperature otherwise the chocolate will set before the sauce can be blended.

For sauces, spoon about two tablespoons of sauce onto a dessert plate. Tip the plate so that the sauce covers the entire bottom. Decorate with a contrasting color. For example, if you are using chocolate sauce, decorate with caramel sauce, raspberry sauce, milk chocolate, or white chocolate. The decorating liquid should be thinner than that used for embossing, but the oil must not ooze out and make a grease mark on the sauce. When decorating with chocolate on chocolate, use oil as a thinner. When decorating with chocolate on an egg, cream, or fruit sauce, use honey as a thinner. Blending can be done using different colors, such as milk chocolate or white chocolate on a dark chocolate glaze, or can even be done with dark chocolate on dark chocolate. This is useful if you are only able to find Passover chocolate chips from the supermarket.

MARBLEIZING

Pipe or drizzle chocolate in circular loops over the sauce. Use a fine-pointed knife or skewer to draw through the loops to make swirls.

HEARTS AND VINES

Use a ⅛-inch teaspoon to place small drops of decorating liquid on wet glaze or sauce. Draw a fine knife tip, skewer, or toothpick through the center of each drop to form hearts. For vines, continue down through other droplets so the hearts connect to form vines.

HERRINGBONE

(1) Pipe parallel lines, ¼ inch apart, vertically across the cake leaving ¼ inch at each side (*see illustration 14.9*).

(2) Turn the cake so that the stripes are now horizontal (*see illustration 14.10*).

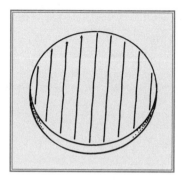

14.9

(3) Starting from the top right or left of the cake, ¼ inch from the edge, and using a very fine knife tip or skewer, draw a vertical line through the piped lines of chocolate. Use a very light touch so that the line in the glaze does not show, but the contrasting piped lines of glaze smudge to make a series of connected chevrons.

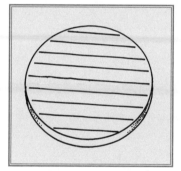

14.10

(4) For the next line start at the bottom, ¼ inch from the line that you just drew, and draw the knife tip upwards to the top of the cake (you have just repeated the first action but in a different direction). The chevrons will be facing the opposite direction (*see illustration 14.11*).

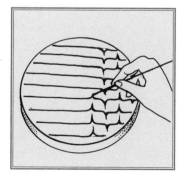

14.11

(5) Continue alternating passes until ¼ inch from the edge. The entire cake should now be covered with a design similar to a herringbone pattern.

For cakes smaller than eight inches, or when decorating sauced plates, the spacing can be changed.

PETAL DESIGNS

Petal designs are made using the same technique as the herringbone design, but the design radiates out from the center of a circle.

(1) Begin by piping concentric circles on top of a round cake. Start in the center with a dot. The last circle should be about ¼ inch from the edge of the cake.

(2) Using a very fine knife tip or skewer draw a straight, shallow line from the center of the cake to the outer edge.

(3) The second line will go from the outer edge toward the center and should be about 1½ inch from the first line (*see illustration 14.12*).

(4) Continue alternating the direction of the draw until the whole cake is marked (*see illustration 14.13*).

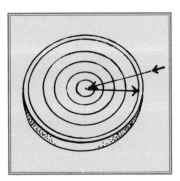

14.12

14.13

SPIDER WEBS

Spider webs are made exactly like petal designs, except that after the rings are piped, the knife is only pulled from the center of the cake to the outer edge.

BLENDING CHOCOLATE

Microwave on medium for 30 seconds or until the chips are shiny and have begun to melt. Stir. If necessary, continue to microwave in 10-second bursts, stirring between heating, until the chips are completely melted and the liquid is smooth, with no lumps of chocolate remaining. Some chocolates will require another teaspoon of oil to make them suitable for blending. To test, place a small pool of glaze on a plate. Pipe a line or two of blending chocolate and draw a skewer through the chocolate to see if the blending chocolate flows smoothly.

2 ounces semisweet Passover chocolate

1 to 2 teaspoons of honey or oil (or both)

187

Chocolate Gratings, Curls, Cigarettes, Etc.

Chocolate decorations melt very easily and should not be touched by hand. Use toothpicks to move decorations so that your body heat does not melt them. Store decorations in the refrigerator between sheets of waxed paper, in an airtight container.

Gratings and Ground Chocolate

Ground chocolate can be made using a food processor and the grating disk. Refrigerate the chocolate so it is very hard. Place in the feed tube with a grating disk in the work bowl, and turn on the processor. Press down on the feed tube, and process until all of the chocolate is grated. Remove the grater and put the metal blade in. Process until the chocolate is finely ground. For small quantities, rub a cold bar of chocolate over a box grater. Catch the gratings on aluminum foil. Fine gratings or flakes can be made using a vegetable peeler and a cold block of chocolate.

Chocolate Leaves

Choose waxy or thick-skinned leaves that are not poisonous. Leave a little bit of stem on to make it easier to peel off the leaf from the chocolate. Rinse with water and dry. Melt the chocolate. Use a small spatula or artist's brush to place the chocolate on the back of the leaf. Put on a thick layer of chocolate. Refrigerate or freeze the leaf until the chocolate is firm. Peel off the leaf starting at the stem end. Refrigerate until ready to use.

Curls and Cigarettes

If you buy slab chocolate (see source 8, page 198) you can place it in a pan, heat it with a gooseneck lamp, and then follow the directions for the different kinds of decorations below. You might want to consult Alice Medrich's book *Cocolat* (see bibliography) for more detailed instructions.

Because the most readily available chocolate for Passover will be chips, the following method uses melted chocolate that will need to be scraped off of another surface. The typical surface to use is the back of a cookie sheet. However, after trying this on all of the pans that I own, I found that little bits of aluminum or other metal ended up in the chocolate. Even the marble slab I own was not useful because it has a coating on it. The only surface that worked for me was glass. The only drawback with using glass is that the decorations are dull. This is certainly preferable to metal in the chocolate. Melt about 6 ounces of chocolate for each 12 × 15-inch pan used (melting directions on page 11). Warm the glass dish with a hair dryer.

Spread the chocolate $^{1}/_{16}$ inch thick on the back of the glass dish (an offset spatula is handy for this). Refrigerate the pan to harden the chocolate (at least 20 minutes).

Remove the pans from the refrigerator and let warm up until soft enough to scrape. The chocolate should neither splinter nor gum up. Chill or allow to soften until the chocolate will do what you want.

FOR CURLS: Scrape the chocolate with a cookie cutter, spoon, or knife held at 90 degrees.

FOR CIGARETTES: Use a spatula or knife held at 45 degrees. Start 2 inches up from the end of the pan (nearest your body) and pull toward your body. To make fatter cigarettes, start farther from the end of the pan. To get longer cigarettes, use a longer knife.

For other shapes and techniques, such as two-tone curls, fans, and ribbons, see *Cocolat* (see bibliography).

189

Cutting Cakes
Horizontal Cutting to Make Multiple Layers

Tender cakes might need to be frozen slightly before they can be cut horizontally into layers. Fifteen minutes to one hour is usually sufficient. Use a serrated knife that is longer than the width of the cake so that you can slice all the way through and see where you are in the cake. Begin by making a shallow ($^{1}/_{16}$ inch) groove all the way around the perimeter of the cake as a marker to show where you want the cut to be and as a "track" that the knife can follow as you cut. To make this groove you can either turn the cake on a decorating turntable or turn the cake until the whole thing is marked. Hold the cake or cake board and begin to cut through the groove with a sawing and rocking motion. If the knife is long enough you will be able to check that the knife is following the groove on all sides. If the top layer that you have just cut is tender, it will be difficult to move it off of the bottom layer. Holding the back edge of the layer, slide a cake board or cookie sheet between the two layers and lift up.

Cutting Cakes into Serving Pieces

Cakes with sticky centers or coatings are sometimes hard to cut into serving pieces that are attractive and unmarred. Usually these types of cakes need to be cut with nonserrated knives. Make sure to use a knife that is long enough to cut all the way across the width the cake. These cakes are also best cut in the kitchen, before serving. To begin, have a pitcher of hot water, a damp cloth, and a dry dish towel near the work surface. Proceed as follows:

(1) Make the first cut. Tilt the blade side to side to make a space for the knife to come out without marring the surface. The knife can be either brought straight up or slid toward the front until clear of the cake. This will be determined by the size of the opening you have made and the thickness of the blade.

(2) Wipe the blade with the damp cloth and dry with the towel.

(3) Continue cutting, rocking, wiping, and drying. When the cloth has no clean place left with which to wipe the knife, dip it in the pitcher of hot water to clean it, wring, and continue.

Sticky round cakes should not be cut to the center, but cut in half, then quarters, eighths, etc., until the desired size is achieved. For an attractive presentation, the wedges can then be arranged back into a circle with a small space between each wedge.

To cut cakes into squares, rectangles, or triangles, make all of the vertical cuts first. If the cake is longer than the knife, make a space after one of the vertical cuts so that the horizontal cut can be made through a section. To make triangles, move each square so that the knife can cut across the square cleanly to make two triangles. Arrange the pieces decoratively on a plate and serve.

Decorating with Fruits

Pears, peaches, and apples turn brown once they are peeled. To help retard browning, squeeze a couple of lemons into a pot of water, and add the fruit to the water as you peel them. Once all of the fruit has been peeled and cut, squeeze another lemon over the cut slices. Glazing helps to keep fruit fresh looking and adds a decorative shine. A simple glaze is used for fruits that are prepared up to three hours ahead of time. For longer storage, use stabilized glaze.

191

½ cup jelly or jam

1 tablespoon Passover wine or water

Fruit Glaze

CURRANT JELLY IS A GOOD CHOICE FOR GLAZING RED FRUITS AS IT DOES NOT INTERFERE WITH THE TASTE OF THE FRUIT. APPLE JELLY IS VERY GOOD FOR WHITISH FRUITS SUCH AS PEARS AND APPLES.

Heat the jelly and water or wine until it melts and starts to simmer. If there are any lumps, strain. Brush warm glaze over fruit.

Stabilized Fruit Glaze

¹/₂ cup jelly

1 tablespoon Passover wine or water

¹/₂ teaspoon Passover gelatin

1 tablespoon cold water

1. Heat jelly and water as in "Fruit Glaze" recipe.

2. Whisk the gelatin into the cold water. Heat in the microwave on high, or in a pan of simmering water, until the gelatin melts (30 seconds in the microwave). Bring the jelly back to a simmer and add the melted gelatin. Brush on fruit immediately.

Unlike regular gelatin, Passover gelatin begins to set very rapidly.

To use regular gelatin, see directions on page 14.

Cutting Fruits

PEARS

For all designs use five to six peeled pears for the top of a 9- or 10-inch dessert.

1. Daisy design: Halve and core very ripe pears. Place narrow ends toward the center *(see illustration 14.14)*.

2. Design two: Halve and core poached pears (recipes on pages 167–69) Slice halves horizontally into very thin slices, not cutting completely through the pear, so that the pear halves remain intact. Place on dessert with narrow ends toward center. Press down on pear to fan the slices.

14.14

14.15

PEARS OR PEACHES

1. Carnation design: (a) Halve, core, and cut the fruit vertically into thin slices.

(b) Place the first row around the outside edge of the dessert with the tips perpendicular to the perimeter of the dessert. Slightly overlap slices *(see illustration 14.15)*.

(c) Place the second row closer to the center, overlapping the tips of the first row. Continue moving toward the center until all but a circle in the center is covered (pears will only have two rows) *(see illustration 14.16)*.

(d) Fill the center with a Pear Flower (page 171) or with two small slices with straight sides touching so they look like a pear or peach, or with a thinly sliced, rolled piece of fruit.

14.16

14.17

2. Rose design: (a) Halve, core, and cut the fruit horizontally into thin slices.

(b) Place the first row with the rounded edge of each slice to the outside edge of the dessert and slices tip to tip *(see illustration 14.17)*.

14.18

(c) Place the second row slightly overlapping the first but have the center of each slice at the junction where two slices of the previous row meet *(see illustration 14.18)*.

(d) Continue toward the center until the whole top is covered. Fill the center with a pear flower (page 171), with two small slices touching to form a peach or pear shape, or with a thinly sliced, rolled piece of fruit.

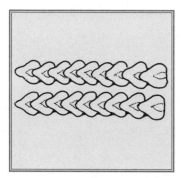

14.19

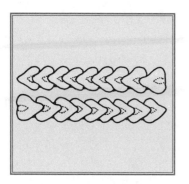

14.20

STRAWBERRIES

For all strawberry designs, remove the stems. Use two pints for a 9- to 10-inch top.

Design 1: Place whole berries around top of dessert so that berries touch each other and cover entire top.

Design 2: Halve berries and place flat side down with berries touching each other. Cover the entire top of the dessert.

Design 3: Slice berries horizontally into rounds or ovals. These can be placed like the other round-oval fruits (see bananas and oranges, pages 196 and 197), or mounded haphazardly.

Design 4: Striped design: (a) Slice berries vertically and place with the tips parallel to the edge of the dessert. Overlap berries slightly.

(b) For the second row the tips can face the same direction as the first, or the opposite direction *(see illustrations 14.19 and 14.20)*.

(c) Continue moving toward the center until the whole dessert is covered.

195

14.21

Design 5: Starburst design: (a) Slice berries vertically and place with the tips perpendicular to the edge *(see illustration 14.21)*.

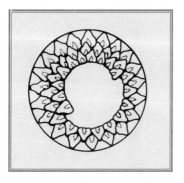

14.22

(b) Place the second row slightly overlapping the first, with the tips placed between two berries of the previous row *(see illustration 14.22)*.

(c) Continue toward the center until the whole top is covered.

BLUEBERRIES AND RASPBERRIES

Wash and drain. Use two pints for a 9- to 10-inch top. Blueberries and raspberries can be placed in rows or mounded haphazardly

BANANAS

Cut into rounds or ovals. Ovals are made by slicing across the banana on the diagonal. Slices can be placed side by side or over-lapping. Ovals can be placed perpendicular or parallel to the cake edge (see strawberry designs).

14.23

14.24

14.25

ORANGES

Use thick-skinned oranges, peel and remove pith (white part).

1. Chrysanthemum design: Slice oranges horizontally (not tip to tip). Overlap slices and place in overlapping circles from the outside edge towards the center. Place an orange slice in the center *(see illustration 14.23)*.

2. Rose design: Slice oranges as above. Continue as in the pear rose pattern, page 194.

3. Wheel design: (a) Cut oranges into slices as in the chrysanthemum design, and then into quarters *(see illustartion 14.24)*.

(b) Place the quarters in rows, with tips toward the center, each quarter touching the other, radiating out from the center like the spokes of a wheel *(see illustration 14.25)*.

197

Appendix

EQUIPMENT AND INGREDIENT SUPPLIERS

1. Bridge Kitchenware
214 East 52nd St.
New York, NY 10022
800/BRIDGE-K
Fax 212/758-5387
www.bridgekitchenware.com

Extensive collection of baking equipment including excellent cake pans, tart pans, whisks, pastry bags, spatulas, and cookie cutters.

2. Sweet Celebrations (formerly Maid of Scandinavia)
3244 Raleigh Ave.
Minneapolis, MN 55416
800/328-6722
Fax 612/927-6215
www.sweetc.com

Extensive collection of candy- and cake-making equipment, books, and foods. Especially good for cake boards, parchment and doilies, vanilla beans, and thermometers.

3. www.kosher4passover.com

Complete line of kosher foods for Passover including chocolate, canned goods, cocoa, almond paste, jams, potato flakes, etc.

4. King Arthur Flour Company
P.O. Box 876
Norwich, VT 05055
800/827-6836
Fax 800/343-3002
www.kingarthurflour.com

Vanilla beans, ground vanilla beans, spices, and nuts, including skinned hazelnuts.

5. Williams-Sonoma
Mail Order Department
P.O. 7456
San Francisco, CA 94120-7456
800/541-2233
www.williams-sonoma.com

Excellent baking pans, whisks, food mills, and strainers, etc.

6. Chef's Catalog
800/338-3232
www.chefscatalog.com

Strainers, parchment paper, cookie sheets in three sizes, jelly roll pans, bundt pans.

7. Kitchenaid
800/541-6330
www.kitchenaid.com

Parts department for ordering extra bowls and stainless steel beaters.

8. Gourmail
800/366-5900, ext. 96
www.gourmail.com

Fine slab chocolate including pareve, kosher for Passover chocolate (minimum order 20 pounds).

9. www.koshersupermarket.com
877/499-9366

Complete line of kosher foods, including chocolate, cocoa, spices, hazelnuts (filberts), and almond paste.

10. The Home Economist
5410 East Independence Blvd.
Charlotte, NC 29212
704/536–HOME
Fax 704/536-2246

Pixie bun pan; all nuts, including hulled hazelnuts; spices and vanilla beans (bulk foods like these are not kosher).

11. www.kitchenkapers.com
800/455-5567

Variety of kitchen equipment including Dupont Teflon mats.

Bibliography

Beranbaum, Rose Levy. *The Cake Bible.* New York: William Morrow and Company, 1988.

Central Conference of American Rabbis. *Gates of the Seasons: A Guide to the Jewish Year.* New York: Central Conference of American Rabbis, 1983.

Child, Julia, Louisette Bertholle, and Simone Beck. *Mastering the Art of French Cooking.* Vol. 2. New York: Alfred A. Knopf, 1961.

Clayton, Bernard, Jr. *The Complete Book of Pastry, Sweet and Savory.* New York: Simon and Schuster, 1981.

Hyman, Philip, and Mary Hyman, trans. *The Best of Gaston Lenotre's Desserts.* New York: Barron's, 1978.

Medrich, Alice. *Cocolat.* New York: Warner Books, 1990.

Purdy, Susan. *As Easy As Pie.* New York: Athenium, 1984.

Strassfeld, Michael. *The Jewish Holidays: A Guide and Commentary.* New York: Harper and Row, 1985.

Wilton Enterprises. The Wilton Way of Cake Decorating. Vol. 3. Woodridge, IL: Wilton Enterprises, 1979.

Index

Almond
  Cheesecake Bars, Chocolate, 46
  Cherry Layer Cake, 108
  Cookie(s)
    Apricot Petit Fours, 27
    Chewy or Crunchy, 31
    Crust, Crunchy, 52
    Sandies, 24
  Sponge Cake, 81
  Tortes, Pear Flower, 94
Almost Seven Layer Cake, 126
Apple Crisp, 69
Apple Tangerine Crisp, 68
Apricot
  Almond Petit Fours, 27
  Chocolate Mini-Tarts, 73
  Filling, 145
  Walnut Pavé, 110
Assorted Mini-Tarts, 72

Baking pans, 4, 5
Banana Berry Sauce, 165
Banana decorations, 196
Bars, Chocolate Almond Cheesecake, 46
Berry Sauce, Banana, 165
Berry Sauce, Orange, 165
Black Forest Cake, 112
Blended designs, 184–86
Blueberry(-ies)
  decorations, 196
  and Lemon Curd Mini-Tarts, 72
  in Red and Blue Nut Tart, 66
Browned Butter Strawberry Tart, 74
Brownies, Pecan Chocolate Chip, 37
Brown Sugar Cake, Strawberry, 104
Brown Sugar Frosting, Sabayon, 137
Butter
  Browned, Strawberry Tart, 74
  nut, about, 16
  Pecan Roll, Chocolate, 114
Buttercream Frosting
  frosting, meringue, about, 130
  Marshmallow Meringue and, 131

Cake boards and pans, 5–6

Cakes
  chocolate. *See* Cholcolate, Cake
  Cocoa Cake Roll, 86
  cutting, 189–91
  Génoise, Passover, 77
  Ladyfingers, 83
  Layer
    Almond Cherry, 108
    Almost Seven Layer, 126
    Apricot Walnut Pavé, 110
    Black Forest, 112
    Chocolate Butter Pecan Roll, 114
    Chocolate Mousse, 106
    Chocolate Noisette layer, 117
    Hazelnut Custard, 118
    Pareve Chocolate Peanut Butter, 102
    Strawberry Brown Sugar, 104
    Tiramisu, 121
    Tiramisu, Peach Raspberry, 123
  Sponge, Almond, 81
  Spongy Base Layer, 85
Caramel
  Cheesecake Squares, 42
  Poached Pears, 167
  Sauce, 163
    Cream, Pear, 164
  Tart, Pecan, 63
  Topping, 146
  Torte, Chocolate Peanut Butter, 99
Cheesecake
  Bars, Chocolate Almond, 46
  Cherry, 44
  Squares
    Caramel, 42
    Lemon Chocolate Marbled, 49
    Strawberry Sour Cream, 39
Cherry(-ies)
  Cheesecake, 44
  Chocolate Mini-Tarts, 72
  Filling, Marinated, 141
  Layer Cake, Almond, 108
  Marinated, and Sauce, 157
Chewy or Crunchy Almond Cookies, 31
Chocolate, 10–11
  Almond Cheesecake Bars, 46

Apricot Mini-Tarts, 73
blending, 187
Cake
  Black Forest, 112
  Butter Pecan Roll, 114
  Mousse, 106
  Noisette Layer, 117
  Peanut Butter, Pareve, 102
  Pecan, 79
Cherry Mini-Tarts, 72
Chip
  Cocoa Pecan Softies, 36
  Cookies, 34
  Pecan Brownies, 37
curls and cigarettes, 188–89
Frosting
  Ganache Glaze and, 148
  Noisette Fluff, Chocolate Flake, 134
  Sabayon, 135
gratings and ground, 187–88
leaves, 188
Marbled Cheesecake Squares, Lemon, 49
Mousse
  Dark, Easy, 150
  Neoclassic, 139
  Stuffed Whole Pears or Quarters, 176
Sauce
  Dark, 162
  Dark, Pareve, 158
  Light, Pareve, 159
Torte
  Fudge, 89
  Peanut Butter Caramel, 99
  Raspberry, 96
  Raspberry Silk, 91
  Strawberry, 96
  Whipped Cream, 147
Cobbler, Pear Pineapple, 70
Cocoa
  Cake Roll, 86
  Chocolate Chip Pecan Softies, 36
  Coconut Macaroons, 25
Coconut, 11–12
  Macaroons, Cocoa, 25
  and Pecan Cookies, 30

Cookie(s)
  Almond
    Apricot Petit Fours, 27
    Chewy or Crunchy, 31
    Crust, Crunchy, 52
    Sandies, 24
  Chocolate Chip, 34
  Cocoa Coconut Macaroons, 25
  Coconut and Pecan, 30
  Crumb Crusts, 52
  Hazelnut Sandwich, 22
  Lemon Nutmeg, 35
  Linzer Tart, 32
  Orange Ginger Sugar, 35
  Pecan Sandies, 24
Couplers, 179
Cream
  Pastry (Crème Patissière), 151
  Sauce, Caramel Pear, 164
  Whipped, 147
    Chocolate, 147
    Roasted Nut, 147
Crème Anglaise, 160
Crème Patissière, 151
  Double Rich, 151
  Low-Fat, 151
Crisp
  Apple, 69
  Apple Tangerine, 68
  Pear Vanilla, 69
  Rhubarb, 69
Crisp Meringue Disks and Tart Shells, 59
Crunchy Almond Cookie Crust, 52
Crusts, pastry. See Pastry(-ies), crusts
Curd, Lemon, 144
Custard and Fresh Fruit Mini-Tarts, 72
Custard Cake, Hazelnut, 118

Dark Chocolate Sauce, 162
Decorating equipment and techniques,
    178–97
  blended designs, 184–86
  chocolate curls and cigarettes, 188–89
  chocolate gratings and ground chocolate,
    187–88
  chocolate leaves, 188
  cutting cakes, 189–91
  embossed designs, 183
  fruits, 191–97
  pastry bags and couplers, 179
  piping, 180–83
  sauce and glaze decorations, 183–87

Dietary guidelines, 1–3

Easy Dark Chocolate Mousse, 150
Egg(s), 12–13
  whites, about, 13
  yolks, about, 14
Embossed designs, 183
Equipment, 4–9. See also Decorating equip-
    ment and techniques

Filling
  Apricot, 145
  Marinated Cherry, 141
  Peanut Butter Mousse, 153
  Raspberry, 142
  Strawberry, 143
Fleur-de-lis, piping, 182
Frosting
  Ganache Glaze and, 148
  Meringue Buttercream, about, 130
  Noisette Fluff, 134
  Sabayon Brown Sugar, 137
  Sabayon Chocolate, 135
Fruit(s)
  decorations using, 192–97
  Glaze, 191
    Stabilized, 192
Fudge, Chocolate, Torte, 89

Ganache Frosting and Glaze, 148
Gelatin, about, 14
Génoise, Passover, 77
Ginger Orange Sugar Cookies, 35
Glaze
  decorations, 183–87
  Fruit, 191
    Stabilized, 192
  Ganache Frosting and, 148
"Graham Cracker" Crust, 53

Hazelnut(s)
  Custard Cake, 118
  Sandwich Cookies, 22
  skinning, 16
Hearts and vines designs, 184
Herringbone decorations, 185–86

Ingredients, 10–18

Jams and jellies, 14–15

Kashering utensils and equipment, 4–5

Ladyfingers, 83
Layer cakes. See Cakes, Layer
Lemon
  Chocolate Marbled Cheesecake Squares, 49
  Curd, 144
    and Blueberry Mini-Tarts, 72
  Nutmeg Cookies, 35
Linzer Tart Cookies, 32
Low-cholesterol recipes, 19
  Apple Tangerine Crisp, 68
  Apricot Filling, 145
  Caramel Poached Pears, 167
  Chocolate Apricot Mini-Tarts, 73
  Chocolate Cherry Mini-Tarts, 72
  Chocolate Sauce, Dark, Pareve, 158
  Chocolate Sauce, Light, Pareve, 159
  Cocoa Chocolate Chip Pecan Softies, 36
  Cookie Crumb Crusts, 52
  Crisp Meringue Disks and Tart Shells, 59
  "Graham Cracker" Crust, 53
  Hazelnut Sandwich Cookies, 22
  Marinated Cherries and Sauce, 157
  Marinated Cherry Filling, 141
  Noisette Fluff Frosting, 134
  Nut Crumb Crust, 55
  Pear Pineapple Cobbler, 70
  Pecan or Almond Sandies, 24
  Raspberry Sauce, 156
  Raspberry Vanilla Mini-Tarts, 72
  Strawberry Filling, 143
  Strawberry Puree and Sauce, 155
  Streusel Topping, 61
  Vanilla Poached Pears, 169
  Wine Poached Pears, 169

Macaroons, Cocoa Coconut, 25
Marbleizing technique, 184
Margarine, about, 15
Marinated Cherries and Sauce, 157
Marinated Cherry Filling, 141
Marshmallow Meringue and Buttercream, 131
Matzo cake meal, about, 15
Meringue
  and Buttercream, Marshmallow, 131
  Buttercream frosting, about, 130
  Disks and Tart Shells, Crisp, 59
Mousse
  Chocolate
    Cake, 106
    Dark, Easy, 150
    Neoclassic, 139
    Stuffed Whole Pears or Quarters, 176

INDEX

Peanut Butter, Filling, 153

Neoclassic Chocolate Mousse, 139
Noisette
  Fluff Frosting, 134
  Layer Cake, Chocolate, 117
  Stuffed Pear Daisies, 174
Nutmeg Lemon Cookies, 35
Nut(s), 15
  butters, about, 16
  Crumb Crust, 55
  grinding, 16
  Roasted, Whipped Cream, 147
  Tart, Red and Blue, 66

Orange
  Berry Sauce, 165
  decorations, 197
  Ginger Sugar Cookies, 35

Pareve Chocolate Peanut Butter Cake, 102
Pareve Dark Chocolate Sauce, 158
Pareve Light Chocolate Sauce, 159
Passover Génoise, 77
Pastry bags, 7, 179
Pastry brushes, 7–8
Pastry Cream (Créme Patissiére), 151
Pastry(-ies)
  crusts
    Cookie Crumb, 52
    "Graham Cracker," 53
    Nut Crumb, 55
    Sweet, 56
  Pecan Caramel Tart, 63
Pavé, Apricot Walnut, 110
Peach(es)
  decorations, 193–94
  Melba Torte, 97
  Tiramisu, Raspberry, 123
Peanut Butter
  Cake, Pareve Chocolate, 102
  Caramel Torte, Chocolate, 99
  Mousse Filling, 153
Pear(s)
  Chocolate Mousse Stuffed Whole, or
    Quarters, 176
  Cream Sauce, Caramel, 164
  Daisies, Noisette Stuffed, 174
  decorations, 192–94
  Flower Almond Tortes, 94
  Flowers, 171
  Nut Tart, 67
  Pineapple Cobbler, 70
  Poached
    Caramel, 167

Vanilla, torte, 98
Vanilla or Wine, 169
Vanilla Crisp, 69
Pecan
  Caramel Tart, 63
  Chocolate Cake, 79
  Chocolate Chip Brownies, 37
  and Coconut Cookies, 30
  Crumb Crust, 55
  Roll, Butter, Chocolate, 114
  Sandies, 24
    Crust, 52
  Softies, Cocoa Chocolate Chip,
    36
Petal designs, 186
Petit Fours, Almond Apricot, 27
Pineapple Pear Cobbler, 70
Piping, 180–83
Potato starch, about, 16–17
Puree, Strawberry, 155

Raspberry(-ies)
  decorations, 196
  Filling, 142
  in Red and Blue Nut Tart, 66
  Sauce, 156
  Tiramisu, Peach, 123
  Torte, Chocolate, 96
  Torte, Silk, Chocolate, 91
  Vanilla Mini-Tarts, 72
Red and Blue Nut Tart, 66
Rhubarb Crisp, 69
Roasted Nut Whipped Cream, 147
Roll, Chocolate Butter Pecan, 114
Rosettes, piping, 182

Sabayon Brown Sugar Frosting, 137
Sabayon Chocolate Frosting, 135
Sandies
  Almond, 24
  Pecan, 24
    Crust, 52
Sauce
  Banana Berry, 165
  Caramel, 163
    Cream, Pear, 164
  Chocolate
    Dark, 162
    Dark, Pareve, 158
    Light, Pareve, 159
  Crème Anglaise, 160
  Marinated Cherries and, 157
  Orange Berry, 165
  Raspberry, 156
  Strawberry Puree and, 155

Shells, piping, 181–82
Softies, Cocoa Chocolate Chip Pecan, 36
Sour Cream Cheesecake, Strawberry, 39
Spider webs, 187
Sponge Cake, Almond, 81
Spongy Base Layer, 85
Squares,Cheesecake
  Caramel, 42
  Lemon Chocolate Marbled, 49
Stabilized Fruit Glaze, 192
Stars, piping, 181
Strawberry
  Brown Sugar Cake, 104
  decorations, 195–96
  Filling, 143
  Puree and Sauce, 155
  Sour Cream Cheesecake, 39
  Tart, Browned Butter, 74
  Torte, Chocolate, 96
Streusel Topping, 61
Sugar Cookies, Orange Ginger, 35
Sweet Pastry Crust, 56

Tangerine Apple Crisp, 68
Tart(s)
  Browned Butter Strawberry, 74
  Mini-, Assorted, 72
  Nut, Red and Blue, 66
  Pecan Caramel, 63
  Shells, Crisp Meringue, 59
Tips and tubes, pastry bag, 180–83
Tiramisu, 121
  Peach Raspberry, 123
Topping, Caramel, 146
Torte(s)
  Chocolate
    Fudge, 89
    Peanut Butter caramel, 99
    Raspberry, 96
    Raspberry Silk, 91
    Strawberry, 96
  Peach Melba, 97
  Pear Flower Almond, 94
  Vanilla Poached Pear, 98

Vanilla, 17–18
  Poached Pears, 169
    Torte, 98
  Raspberry Mini-Tarts, 72

Walnut Apricot Pavé, 110
Whipped Cream, 147
  Chocolate, 147
  Roasted Nut, 147
Wine Poached Pears, 169